Universities and Their Cities

UNIVERSITIES AND THEIR CITIES

Urban Higher Education in America

STEVEN J. DINER

Johns Hopkins University Press
BALTIMORE

Printed in the United States of America on acid-free paper
9 8 7 6 5 4 3 2

Johns Hopkins University Press
2715 North Charles Street
Baltimore, Maryland 21218-4363
www.press.jhu.edu

Library of Congress Cataloging-in-Publication Data

Names: Diner, Steven J., 1944– author.
Title: Universities and their cities : urban higher education in America / Steven J. Diner.
Description: Baltimore, Maryland : Johns Hopkins University Press, 2017. | Includes bibliographical references and index.
Identifiers: LCCN 2016035064 | ISBN 9781421422411 (hardcover : alk. paper) | ISBN 9781421422428 (electronic) | ISBN 1421422417 (hardcover : alk. paper) | ISBN 1421422425 (electronic)
Subjects: LCSH: Urban universities and colleges—United States—History. | Education, Urban—United States—History. | Education, Higher—Social aspects—United States. | Community and college—United States.
Classification: LCC LB2328.42.U6 D56 2017 | DDC 378.73—dc23
LC record available at https://lccn.loc.gov/2016035064

A catalog record for this book is available from the British Library.

Johns Hopkins University Press uses environmentally friendly book materials, including recycled text paper that is composed of at least 30 percent post-consumer waste, whenever possible.

For my grandchildren—Hannah, Abraham, and Emmanuel

Contents

Preface

This book focuses broadly on how higher education practitioners thought about cities and how the urban location of colleges and universities influenced their mission and activities. I examine how these colleges and universities addressed the traditional bias of American colleges in favor of rural areas and the attitudes at these institutions toward students who lived in cities, students who commuted to campus from home, adult students, and students who attended college part-time. Over time, universities in cities increasingly engaged in urban research, using their home cities to broaden their students' education. They also provided various kinds of service to their communities. These universities also had to decide how to relate to the neighborhoods adjacent to their campuses, an issue that became increasingly complex after World War II, as enrollments soared, large numbers of low-income racial minorities moved to many of these neighborhoods, and federal funds became available for urban renewal projects.

This narrative is not limited to particular kinds of institutions. For more than a hundred years, higher educators have debated what it means to be an "urban university" or an "urban college." I discuss how the understanding of this term has changed over time and how in many ways it has stayed the same. Even today, some would argue that elite private universities in cities are not "urban universities." This study is about universities located in cities and is not limited to institutions that meet some set of criteria to be defined as "urban." It includes private institutions, some of which had elite status, as well as municipal universities, state universities, Catholic institutions, and others.

Studying this subject also raises the question of what jurisdictions are defined as cities in different time periods. As the United States became increasingly urban, the populations of major cities grew ever larger, and lists of the nation's largest cities changed with each decennial census. I have not set a minimum size of city population for inclusion in this book. However, I have tended to concentrate on the largest cities. Of course, the boundaries of cities changed significantly over time, and some institutions located outside city limits became important urban institutions after annexation. Over time, cities became the core of extensive metropolitan areas, and many colleges and universities developed outside the city but within the metropolitan area. Metropolitan area colleges and universities have certainly been shaped by the continuing process of urbanization, but I have focused my narrative primarily on central city institutions.

There are, of course, many ways to study the history of universities in cities. One could select a group of institutions as case studies, using their archives, institutional publications, and other sources to illuminate their histories. One might also examine how students viewed their college experiences, relying heavily on oral history interviews, memoirs, and student publications. This would require a selection of specific institutions from the hundreds located in cities. Histories of this kind would greatly illuminate our understanding of this subject, and I hope some historians will undertake such studies in the future. My approach, however, attends to national trends and discussions about how universities could and should connect to their cities.

This narrative looks primarily at colleges and universities with undergraduate programs. Professional schools, especially in law and medicine, emerged largely in cities so that they could have access to hospitals, courts, government agencies, and other entities relevant to professional practice. Many of these schools began as independent entities but later became part of one of their city's universities. However, professional schools, and later many graduate programs, did not have to address the historic bias of American higher education favoring the education of students in rural settings.

Two-year junior colleges, later known as community colleges, expanded rapidly in cities in the latter part of the twentieth century. These institutions have a long and complex history, about which several scholars have written. Given the differences between junior colleges and universities, however, I have limited my history primarily to the latter.

I have been interested in the relationship of universities and cities since the beginning of my academic career. My PhD dissertation and my first book, *A City and Its Universities: Public Policy in Chicago, 1892–1919*, was devoted to this subject, as were several of my other publications. I started my academic career at the University of the District of Columbia (then called Federal City College), a new municipal university serving students in Washington, DC, where I taught urban studies for thirteen years. In 1998, I became the dean of arts and sciences at Rutgers University–Newark, and four years later I became chancellor, a position I held for ten years. In these leadership roles, I worked to develop Rutgers University–Newark as a leading urban research university and to engage students and faculty with the city of Newark. I also participated actively in national urban university organizations and served as president of the Coalition of Urban and Metropolitan Universities. When I left administration and returned to faculty, I began research on the history of universities' relationship to cities in twentieth-century America.

Many years of involvement with universities in cities has undoubtedly influenced the questions I pose in this book and the answers I present. A historian's background and experiences normally play a role in how that scholar looks at the past. My relationship to the subject of this book, however, is unusually close. This surely has shaped the present volume. I hope that, along with whatever bias it reflects, it has also strengthened my insight into how universities in cities have related to their urban environment.

Acknowledgments

While serving as chancellor of Rutgers University Newark, I knew that at some point I would leave administration and return to the work of a faculty member. Although many former chancellors or presidents do not engage in scholarly research when freed from administrative duties, I looked forward to doing so. Given my previous historical writing and my intense commitment to building Rutgers University Newark as a premier urban research university, I definitely planned to write about the history of urban higher education in America.

At the end of the fall semester of 2011, my chancellorship ended abruptly because I was working aggressively to create a major public university in Newark by merging my institution with the New Jersey Institute of Technology and what was then the main campus of the University of Medicine and Dentistry of New Jersey. The president of Rutgers University, Richard McCormick, saw this potential merger in Newark as a great threat to Rutgers "flagship" campus in New Brunswick and asked for my resignation. As I learned in my research for this book, this kind of mistrust is consistent with the long tradition of anti-urbanism in American higher education. However, I did not need to resume teaching for a year, so I decided to begin work on the history of urban universities.

A longtime friend and colleague, New York University education and history professor Harold Wechsler, assisted me in innumerable ways. He suggested scholarly works relevant to this subject. He pointed me to primary sources and archives. He talked with me at length about the questions I might pose and some of the themes that began to emerge from my research. He introduced me to scholars of the history of higher education. And three years later, when I completed my initial draft, he read the manuscript and made extraordinarily helpful comments.

James Fraser, also from NYU, expressed strong interest in this project, and I discussed my research with him on several occasions. He read a revised draft and provided excellent feedback. Roger Geiger at Penn State University also gave me useful suggestions on several chapters. I had helpful conversations and received strong encouragement from Linda Eisenmann, at Wheaton College, from university presidents who attend the annual meetings of the Coalition of Urban and Metropolitan Universities, and from scholars at the History of Education Society conferences.

Gregory Britton, editorial director of Johns Hopkins University Press, expressed keen interest in this project early in my research, and he stayed in contact over several years, encouraging me to submit my completed manuscript to Johns Hopkins. It has been a great pleasure working with him. I greatly appreciate his encouragement and support. Catherine Goldstead at the Press has been very helpful in preparing the book's photographs.

Natalie Borisovets, librarian at Dana Library of Rutgers University Newark, has assisted me in numerous ways. Lee Hiltzik helped me navigate the extensive materials at the Rockefeller Archives. I also want to thank the archivists at the Hoover Institution, the Rockefeller Archives, and the archives at Hunter College, Columbia University, and the University of Wisconsin–Milwaukee. Amy Weiss aided me in acquiring the book's photographs, and Glenn Perkins provided excellent editing.

I want to give special thanks to Chancellor Nancy Cantor, my successor at Rutgers University Newark. She and I share a vision of how universities should engage with their cities, and she has provided excellent leadership to our institution. She has also strongly encouraged me to pursue this project and has provided significant support for my research.

Finally, I am grateful to my wife, Hasia R. Diner, for her enthusiastic encouragement and her continuing love and devotion.

Universities and Their Cities

1

The Collegiate Ideal and Nineteenth-Century Cities

In 1883, Charles F. Thwing, a minister with deep interest in higher education, published a study of American colleges. In his chapter 3, entitled "Morals," he asserted that a significant number of city-bred college students "are immoral on their entering college" because the city environment has "for many of them been excellent preparatory schools for Sophomoric dissipation" and "even home influences . . . have failed to outweigh the evil attractions of the gambling table and its accessories." In contrast, students from rural settings have been deeply elevated by "not only the purity of the student's home but the associations of his country life." Moreover, he explained, the higher rates of immorality among students in colleges "located in or near cities" reflected "the character and surroundings of the colleges."[1]

American cities, about which Thwing expressed deep concern, had grown rapidly throughout the nineteenth century, even as large numbers of Americans moved west to new states and territories. Atlantic ports, founded in the colonial era to facilitate the movement of people and goods to and from Britain, remained crucial to the economy and grew rapidly. The nation's continuing expansion required commercial centers in towns and cities inland where merchants could buy and sell goods to rural residents. These towns served as links in the emerging transportation system. Later in the century, manufacturing enterprises located in cities because of their advantages in transporting materials to factories and manufactured goods to consumers throughout the country.

The first US census, taken in 1790, and those censuses in subsequent decades defined a city as a jurisdiction of at least 2,500 residents. As the overall US population grew, cities grew much more rapidly. In 1820, one of fourteen Americans lived in cities as defined by the census. By 1860, the number rose to approximately one in five, and by 1900 over one in three. The 1880 census for the first time sought to identify more substantially sized cities by recognizing communities with 8,000 residents or more. This standard classified 22.5 percent of the 1880 population as urban.[2]

The population of large cities also expanded over the course of the nineteenth century. In 1820, only 12 cities had populations of 10,000 or more. By 1860, that number had grown to 101 cities, and 8 cities reached 100,000. By 1900, New York City housed just under 3.5 million people; Chicago, 1.7 million; and Philadelphia, 1.3 million. St. Louis, Boston, and Baltimore each had over 500,000, and Cleveland, Buffalo, San Francisco, Cincinnati, and Pittsburgh had more than 300,000.

The rapid growth of cities required a host of services to address the issues that grew out of population density. These included paving streets, providing garbage and sewage disposal, addressing the health problems that arose from so many people living near each other, combatting crime, and determining how to deal with the large number of poor people.

Anti-Urbanism in College and in the Nation

Many writers, intellectuals, and government officials expressed deep concern about how the growth of cities could undermine traditional American values. Anti-urbanism dated back to the colonial era and took on special importance after independence, in discussions of the meaning of American "democracy." In 1784, Thomas Jefferson wrote that "the mobs of great cities add just so much to the support of pure government, as sores do to the strength of the human body." Three years later, he assured James Madison that "our governments will remain virtuous for many centuries as long as they are chiefly agricultural." In the 1850s, a writer to the *Prairie Farmer*, published in Chicago, complained that city life "crushes, enslaves and ruins so many thousands of our young men, who are insensibly made the victims of dissipation, of reckless speculation, and of ultimate crime."[3] In 1885, the Reverend Josiah Strong, a prominent leader of a movement to use Protestant religious principles in solving the problems brought on by urbanization, industrialization, and immigration, published *Our Country: Its Possible Future and Its Present Crisis*. In this widely read book, he presented a list of "perils" facing the country, one being "the city," which he described as "a serious menace to our civilization."[4]

Anti-urbanism took on political significance in the election of 1896, when the populist Democratic nominee William Jennings Bryan campaigned against the gold standard. In his famous speech in favor of the free coinage of silver, Bryan dismissed the argument that "the great cities are in favor of the gold standard," asserting: "Burn down your cities and leave our farms and your cities will spring up again as if by magic. But destroy our farms and the grass will grow in the streets of every city in the country."[5]

Urban civic and governmental leaders, whether or not they accepted this negative view of cities, worked to build parks and plant trees in their communities. Advocates for creating a major park in New York City argued that it would improve the health of residents and the behavior of working-class people. The poet William Cullen Bryant, editor of the *New York Evening Post*, called for a new park in an 1844 editorial, arguing that parks contribute "to the health . . . and the morals of the community." In 1853 he asserted that the proposed park would create "fewer inducements to open drinking houses."[6] The first portion of Central Park opened to the public in 1858. Many other cities also built major parks, and a national movement developed to encourage reforestation not only in cities but across the country.[7]

From the beginning of the nineteenth century, leaders of private American colleges, founded largely by Protestant denominations, shared Reverend Thwing's concerns about the negative influence of cities. Like Thwing, Louis A. Dunn, a Baptist minister and president of the Central University of Iowa, published a short history of the American college, in 1876. He concluded, "Colleges located in quiet rural towns, do accomplish more work and better work . . . than in other localities," and "large cities, business centres, places where the people congregate . . . should never be chosen" as a location for a college.[8]

Public college leaders, too, often opposed city locations. The founders and supporters of these colleges believed deeply that college education must build character and spiritual values in the small number of young men who attended public institutions. To inculcate these values colleges should not only isolate students from the negative influences of cities but also surround students with trees, shrubs, and the vegetation of the countryside. Colleges built dormitories, had students eat at campus dining halls, and developed elaborate extracurricular programs to foster a deep sense of institutional community, what historian Frederick Rudolph termed "the collegiate way."[9]

Before winning election as US president, Woodrow Wilson was a professor at, and later president of, Princeton University, an elite, historic institution with a self-contained rural campus. Wilson argued that college should promote "liberal culture" for a select group of men capable of appreciating "moral, intellectual, and aesthetic values." This education prepared them for national service and civic leadership. However, it was not appropriate "for the majority who carry forward the common labor of the world." It could be accomplished only in a "compact and homogeneous" residential college. "You cannot go to college on a streetcar and know what college means," Wilson asserted.[10]

A small number of private women's colleges opened in the nineteenth century, and they also sought to build student character at locations far removed from the negative influences of the city. However, their founders and leaders did not develop rural campuses like those built for men. They believed that women students had to be supervised day and night by college staff, so each institution built a large, self-contained building within which students would live, eat, attend class, and study. In the years after the Civil War, some male institutions started to admit women, and others built separate women's colleges within their institutions.[11]

Private Colleges in Cities and the Rural Ideal

King's College in New York City, now Columbia University, opened in 1754 on lower Broadway. Advocates of a college for the colony of New York had proposed various locations outside of the city, among them Newburgh, Rye, and Hempstead. However, leaders of the Anglican Church thought that a college in New York City would make help make New York the center of the church in North America.[12] The college closed during the revolution but reopened with a new name, Columbia College, in 1784. It moved to Park Place, then to 49th Street and Madison Avenue in 1857. In 1897, it relocated to Morningside Heights in upper Manhattan. In part, the move provided land for substantial expansion. But it also enabled Columbia to remove itself from the central city, to build an enclosed landscaped campus with student housing in a minimally settled area.

In 1755, the College of Philadelphia opened as an extension of a secondary school, the Academy of Philadelphia on Fourth and Arch Streets. In 1801, the college moved to a mansion on Ninth and Market Streets. Like Columbia, its new campus was well beyond the city's development, on land across the Schuylkill River in West Philadelphia. In western Pennsylvania, the Pittsburgh academy, founded in 1787 as a secondary school, began offering baccalaureate instruction in 1819 under the name Western University of Pennsylvania. It had several locations downtown before moving to Observatory Hill on the city's North Side. In 1908, it changed its name again, to the University of Pittsburgh, and moved in 1909 to an undeveloped area in what is now the Oakland neighborhood of Pittsburgh.

New York University has a somewhat different history. It started in 1831 at Clinton Hill near City Hall in lower Manhattan but moved a bit uptown to Washington Square three years later. It began with the avowed purpose of making education available to city residents and developed programs to train lawyers, doctors, nurses, and teachers. Its baccalaureate liberal arts college, however, ceased to attract substantial enrollment in the 1880s. In his annual report to the trustees in 1890, the university's vice chancellor, Henry MacCracken, stated that "the marked advance of business into the neighborhood of the University raises the question whether our work might be advanced by any change of place." The University College (the undergraduate liberal arts school), he continued, planted in some easily accessible neighborhood, "would in a short time fulfill more nearly the American idea of a college than a college in a business locality ever can." The administration considered finding land for a new campus in upper Manhattan, above 150th Street. But it soon decided on a campus more remote from the central city, in an undeveloped area of the Bronx. There, NYU built a thoroughly landscaped residential undergraduate campus on a hill overlooking the Harlem River. The professional programs remained at Washington Square. Interestingly, a few years later, MacCracken, now NYU chancellor, gave a speech advocating an experiment in construction of dormitories in the Washington Square neighborhood to "create a community spirit" not possible for students dispersed beyond the campus. He explained, "Under the wise supervision of fellows and professors," dormitories "may be made a valuable part of even a metropolitan college," thereby counteracting the social isolation thought to be created by city life.[13]

Founders of colleges in the Midwest and New England had similar concerns about urban location. Early nineteenth-century business and civic leaders in the Western Reserve territory, which became the state of Ohio, sought to establish a college, and several towns and villages wanted to have it located in their jurisdiction. One of these was the city of Cleveland. The college founders rejected it because it was a commercial port, which they assumed would have rollicking sailors on its streets, a bad influence on college men. A correspondent following the debate over the college's location argued for the town of Hudson because it "will be retired from the noise and bustle of a commercial city. No sailors will appear to annoy the students. Whilst cities are too often crowded with the unprincipled and immoral, Hudson will probably continue to be peopled by a set of sober, industrious farmers."[14] Western Reserve College did open in Hudson in 1826; at the time it was the only college in northern Ohio. In the next fifty-four years, nine other colleges opened in this region, all in rural locations. As a result, Western Reserve decided to relocate to Cleveland, building a new campus on land, in what at that time was known as "uptown Cleveland," donated by industrialist Amasa Stone. Ironically, Charles Thwing assumed the presidency of this city institution in 1890, eight years after the move to Cleveland. In 1897, he published another book on the American college. This time, however, he argued that cities had significant assets for higher education and weighed these against the advantages of the countryside. He concluded that a college should "not be in the midst of the city, but on its borders—so near that the great life of the town can come into the college . . . and so the students and professors can enter into this great life, helping to qualify it." But the location "should be so near the green fields and forests, that all those delights and all those influences which belong to nature may enter into and possess the quiet or the restless soul."[15]

Washington University in St. Louis, opened in 1853, supported by local business, political, and religious leaders concerned about the limited opportunities for higher education in the Midwest. The trustees named it "Washington Institute" in 1854, in honor of George Washington, changing the name to Washington University two years later. It primarily offered night classes and initially used public buildings. In 1854 it acquired a downtown building at Seventeenth Street and Washington Avenue. In 1890 it moved to a 103-acre campus west of the city limits, in Saint Louis County, known as "Hilltop" because of its beauty and elevation. Indeed, a hilltop location became popular among universities because of its scenic beauty and, in urban institutions, its greater separation from the city.

The founders of Boston University, created in 1869, hoped to locate it in suburban Brookline. But inadequate funds precluded that, so the university over time acquired buildings in the city on Beacon Hill. On the covers of its publications, it quoted Longfellow: "Where should the scholar live? In solitude or in society? In the green stillness of the country, where he can hear the heart of nature beat, or in the dark grey town, where he can hear and feel the throbbing beat of men? I will make answer for him, and say, in the dark grey town."[16] Clearly Boston University's leaders felt the need to justify its urban location.

Relatively few private universities in the South opened in cities. At the request of a cousin from Nashville involved in planning a Methodist Episcopal university in his city, Cornelius Vanderbilt pledged a half million dollars, later increased to $1 million, to establish a university in the general vicinity of Nashville. The university's supervisors seriously considered three sites: two in Edgefield, a separate town east of Nashville across the Cumberland River, and a third on the south side of West End Avenue, an undeveloped area within Nashville's boundaries. One local newspaper argued against the Nashville location, asserting that the city government was concerned only with promoting business and manufacturing and therefore would not support the university. Another newspaper argued that Edgefield "is quieter; it has more of a green sward and leafy wood and the scenic beauties of nature generally," combining "the attractions of country with the conveniences of city." In May 1873, the board of supervisors announced the selection of a seventy-five-acre site in Nashville's West End. A history of Vanderbilt states that for several decades thereafter, "the campus and the area around it were still rural and pristine." Moreover, in designing the campus, the university transplanted large numbers of trees from an adjacent forest.[17]

After the Civil War, former abolitionists and others committed to providing African Americans with education opened colleges for former slaves and other blacks, but they too sought to locate these institutions in a rural environment. Opponents of slavery created the Nashville Normal and Theological Institute during the Civil War to educate freedmen. It moved to a site near the new Vanderbilt campus in 1874 and was renamed Roger Williams University in 1883. One of its early faculty members, the distinguished African American scholar and educator John Hope, extolled the virtues of the country campus because "beyond the college farm not a house was to be seen for miles."[18] The American Missionary Society opened Fisk University in 1866, on property that had housed a veterans hospital and now had a substantial black population. Fisk's trustees acquired land for a larger campus just outside of Nashville in 1873, at a "beautiful twenty five acre site."[19]

Similarly, in 1867 the American Baptist Home Mission Society created the Augusta Institute to educate black men, but the society moved it to Atlanta in 1879, renaming it the Atlanta Baptist Seminary, because it believed it could better serve the people of Georgia in the capital, which was also closer to the state's geographic center. The initial site in Atlanta, adjacent to the railroad station and a lumber mill, proved noisy and offered few places for students to live. So in 1890 it moved to a larger site farther from the city center. George Sale, who assumed the presidency at the time of this move, expressed great interest in the physical beauty of the campus and initiated the planting of a row of twenty-four elm trees at its entrance. His successor in 1896, John Hope, shared this concern for beauty and nature. In 1913, the institution changed its name to Morehouse College.[20] Likewise, the Freedman's Aid Society of the Methodist Episcopal Church founded Clark College in 1869. Chartered in 1877, it moved to a 450-acre site in South Atlanta in 1883. And the African Methodist Episcopal Church founded Morris Brown Colored College, which opened in Atlanta in 1885.

Antislavery activists also pushed for the creation of a college for freedmen in Washington, DC. Howard University opened in 1867 in a temporary building that had housed a beer salon and dance hall. Almost immediately, however, members of the university board began looking for a larger site. They soon purchased land outside what was then the boundary of the city of Washington but within the District of Columbia. A farmer owned the tract called "Smith

Howard University in Washington, D.C., c. 1900. Courtesy of the Library of Congress Prints & Photographs Online Catalog (digital ID cph 3a40804).

farm," which may have been a slave plantation before the Civil War. An article in the local newspaper described the site of the new school as "beautiful," enhanced by "a romantic grove" and "many large gushing springs of sparkling water."[21]

Land-Grant Colleges

In 1862, Congress passed the Morrill Act encouraging the establishment of public land-grant universities in each state by providing them with funds from the sale of public lands. It required the institutions to focus on teaching agriculture and the mechanical arts, but it did not preclude the teaching of classics as well. The mission of the land-grant institutions expanded with the passage of the Hatch Act in 1887, which funded state agricultural experiment stations. States established or designated existing institutions as their land-grant colleges over the next several decades. The land-grant focus on agriculture provided a rationale for the location of these institutions in rural areas, although the other focus on mechanical arts could have supported a city location. Indeed, in Illinois, in response to demands from mechanics in Chicago, the lower house of the state legislature passed a bill providing for a land-grant university in Urbana with a mechanical department in Chicago. In Indiana, civic leaders in Indianapolis urged, unsuccessfully, that a land-grant research center be established in their city, with land-grant professorships distributed among the five existing colleges and universities across the state.

In the end, state governmental leaders located the overwhelming majority of land-grant institutions in rural areas. In Minnesota, after the passage of the Morrill Act, it appeared that the land-grant institution would be created in the town of Glencoe. But in 1867 the state located it in Minneapolis with a "farm campus" for the Agriculture College outside the city. The 1860 census reported 5,809 people living in Minneapolis, a modest population for a city at that time. St. Paul, across the river, had a population of 10,401, making it the eighty-ninth largest city in the United States. Clearly the decision to locate Minnesota's university in Minneapolis did not represent a radical departure from the rural orientation of higher education in the mid-nineteenth century.

In Ohio, substantial debate ensued between advocates of an agricultural institution in a rural area and those who sought a broader institution located in Columbus, the state capital. The editor of the *Ohio State Journal*, James M. Comly, wrote that "no intelligent person professes now to believe that a purely agricultural college . . . would be of any particular benefit to the state."[22] The

Massachusetts Institute of Technology in Boston, 1903. Courtesy of the Library of Congress Prints & Photographs Online Catalog (digital ID pan 6a06371).

Columbus advocates won, and the Ohio Agricultural and Mechanical College opened within the boundaries of the city of Columbus, but in an area that at the time was rural. In 1870, 31,000 people lived in Columbus, the forty-second-largest city population in the United States.

The Massachusetts Institute of Technology, a new institution focused on engineering and science, opened in 1866 in the Back Bay neighborhood of Boston. Rural advocates got the land-grant designation assigned to the proposed Massachusetts Agricultural College (now the University of Massachusetts Amherst), but the founders of MIT secured a portion of the land-grant funds for mechanical arts. It was the only case where land-grant designation went to two different institutions. Popularly known as Boston Tech, MIT remained in Boston until 1916, when it moved across the Charles River to Cambridge.

New Research Universities

In the latter part of the nineteenth century, several new private institutions devoted to advanced research and education of PhDs began to transform American higher education. A huge private endowment made possible the creation of Johns Hopkins University in 1876 in Baltimore. About a decade later, another large endowment created Clark University in Worcester, Massachusetts. A few years after that, John D. Rockefeller funded the University of Chicago, which opened in 1892. The founding presidents of all three institutions recognized that the cultural, industrial, and commercial resources of a city could enhance opportunities for research. Although they enrolled undergraduate students, they were less concerned with traditional views about character building in locations close to nature because they focused on graduate study and research.

Municipal Colleges

Two other kinds of higher education institutions, municipal colleges and Catholic colleges, developed in cities throughout the nineteenth century. These institutions taught mostly commuter students who lived in the city. Municipal universities received much of their money from local government. Some began as private institutions that the city took over. The College of Charleston, chartered in 1785, faced serious financial problems in the late 1820s and early 1830s. The Charleston City Council took control of the college in 1837, providing funding and appointing its trustees. The New York City Board of Education created the Free Academy of New York, now City College, in 1847 for men. In 1870, it established Hunter College, also with free tuition, for women. A bequest to Cincinnati for a free university provided initial funds to found the University of Cincinnati in 1858. In 1870, the Ohio legislature enacted a law allowing cities to establish universities funded by city taxes. The University of Toledo, founded in 1872, was taken over by the city government in 1884.

State governments did not fund many general-purpose colleges or universities in nineteenth-century cities. However, the movement for universal public schooling expanded the need for well-trained teachers, who typically studied at normal schools, both public and private. Many of these institutions began as high schools or programs within high schools but over time some evolved into postsecondary institutions for teacher training, and eventually into four-year colleges. Hunter College, for example, began in 1871 as the Female Normal and High School, renamed the next year the Normal College of the City of New York. Its name changed to Hunter College in 1914 to honor its founding president, Thomas Hunter, who served in that role for thirty-five years.[23] Normal schools emerged across the country, funded by states, counties, and municipalities. State-funded normal schools opened in Baltimore in 1866, Buffalo and Providence in 1871, Boston in 1873, Los Angeles in 1882, Milwaukee in 1885, San Francisco in 1899, and Pittsburgh in 1903.[24] Nearly all of them eventually became or were incorporated into state universities.

Catholic Colleges

Catholic bishops and other church leaders established many colleges in the United States during the nineteenth century. Many of these began as secondary school academies or as seminaries to prepare men for the priesthood, located in serene rural environments where the founders sought to create a monastic atmosphere. But a significant number opened in or near cities, with their leaders often expressing ambivalence about their urban location. Bishop John Carroll established St. Mary's Seminary in Baltimore in 1791. It moved a few years later to an area on the northwest edge of the city. In 1805, Maryland chartered it as a civic college as well. Its undergraduate college became part of the newly opened Loyola College of Maryland, founded in the city in 1852.

In 1818, Missouri's bishop created Saint Louis Academy, a high school. He expanded it in 1820, renaming it Saint Louis College. The Missouri legislature chartered it in 1829, and the bishop persuaded the Jesuit order to run the college. It opened a medical school in 1836 and a law school in 1843. In 1836, its trustees decided that it should move to a location outside the city because housing construction had begun in the neighborhood, and therefore the college would not have a quiet environment. A trustee committee purchased a three-and-a-half-acre farm outside the city and decided that the college should move there. They actually began construction but eventually abandoned the project for financial and other reasons. In 1889, Saint Louis College moved farther from the center city, to an area called Lindall Grove.[25]

Xavier College, founded as a seminary in Cincinnati in 1829, also experienced the effects of city growth several decades later. Unlike Saint Louis College, it did not move farther out. But it eliminated classes after 2:30 p.m. to assist commuting students. The college catalogue for 1886–87 explained, "Owing to the extension of the city into the suburbs, the double session has become an inconvenience to the majority of students who came from a distance, and a hindrance to the proper preparation of classwork at home." The new schedule enabled students "to reach home at a reasonable hour" and provided "the requisite amount of time" for "the preparation of tasks and recitations for the following day."[26]

The second bishop of Boston, Benedict Joseph Fenwick, announced in 1830 his desire to establish a college to serve Catholics in New England. After some unsuccessful efforts to locate the college in Boston, he made plans to open it in in Benedicta, Maine, an experimental agricultural settlement seventy miles north of Bangor, created as a refuge for needy Irish immigrants. Ultimately Fenwick embraced the establishment of a residential college adjacent to a new Catholic secondary school opened on a farm about three miles from the city of Worcester. In 1843, Fenwick began construction of the College of the Holy

Cross.[27] One of Fenwick's successors, Archbishop John Joseph Williams, established the Boston Ecclesiastical Seminary (now St. John's Seminary) in the Brighton neighborhood of Boston in 1884. Jesuits opened Boston College on Harrison Avenue in the city in 1854. Initially a seminary, it began teaching lay students in 1864. In 1907, however, the college purchased thirty-one acres of land in Chestnut Hill in the city of Newton, about six miles from Boston, and it began construction of a new campus in 1909.[28]

One Catholic institution, what is now Fordham University, had its rural campus incorporated into New York City as a result the city's annexation of surrounding territory. The institution opened in 1841 in the Rose Hill area of Westchester County as St. John's College. Fifty-seven years later, in 1898, New York City persuaded the state legislature to incorporate a portion of Westchester County, which included Rose Hill, into an enlarged New York City as the borough of the Bronx. In 1905, it changed its name to Fordham University.

In 1847, St. John's College also opened a unit in New York City, named College of St. Francis Xavier in 1861. Its name also changed in 1905 to Fordham University. Likewise, Manhattan College, initially named the Academy of the Holy Infancy, opened in New York in 1853 and secured a charter as a college from the New York Board of Regents ten years later. Its founders located it at 131st Street and Broadway, well beyond the city's development. In Philadelphia, the nation's second largest city, La Salle College opened in the central city in 1863 but moved to a mansion in an outlying residential area on North Broad Street in 1886.

Many of the Catholic colleges founded in cities remained in the city for the rest of the century and beyond. The College of St. John the Baptist (now St. John's University), operated by Vincentians, opened on Lewis Avenue in the Bedford-Stuyvesant neighborhood of Brooklyn in 1871. It remained there until 1955, when it began relocating to a new campus in Jamaica, Queens. St. Francis College, founded as a secondary school in 1859, began a "literary college" in 1884 on Baltic Street in Brooklyn. It is still located in Brooklyn. Canisius College opened on Washington Street in Buffalo in 1870. Jesuits began the college program of Saint Ignatius College (now the University of San Francisco) in 1859, and another college named for St. Ignatius (now Loyola University Chicago) in 1872 on Chicago's West Side. The Jesuits also established Detroit College (now the University of Detroit) in 1877, Creighton University in Omaha in 1878, and Marquette in Milwaukee in 1881. The

Vincentians founded St. Vincent's College (now DePaul University) on Chicago's North Side in 1898.

Professional Schools

Although the number of urban colleges remained modest, specialized institutions designed to prepare people for the practice of medicine, law, or other professions developed more extensively in nineteenth-century cities. Law students could benefit greatly by proximity to courts and government agencies. Medical practitioners could profit from hospitals or clinics, as well as access to cadavers. Traditionally, aspiring lawyers would "read law" in the offices of a practicing lawyers. They would observe and learn from practitioners. The state did not require any formal education to practice law. And lawyers did not need a baccalaureate degree if they did decide to attend law school. Likewise, medical education lacked any systematic study of science and often did not require a college degree for admission. Rather, medical students observed and worked with practitioners, whom they paid handsomely for the privilege.

Formal education for these professions evolved dramatically in the nineteenth century. Educators viewed the purpose of this kind of professional education quite differently than the goal of character building of gentlemen in undergraduate education. Moreover, adults made up a good number of the students attending urban professional schools, and educators believed that these students, unlike impressionable undergraduates, did not need access to nature. David Starr Jordan, the founding president of Stanford University and a leading figure in higher education, wrote in 1903 that "a college should be in a town so small that college interests overshadow all others." Higher education, he asserted, "mostly begins when a boy goes away from home" but "you cannot get it on the streetcars." However, university professional schools "may be in a great city," Jordan allowed.[29]

Large numbers of medical, law, and other professional schools developed in nineteenth-century cities. Most began as proprietary endeavors, independent of colleges and universities. Instructors charged substantial fees and made a good deal of money. Many of these schools eventually affiliated with established colleges or universities. One scholar estimates that 175 different medical schools offered classes at some point in the first half of the nineteenth century. According to another researcher, thirty-six distinct law schools operated before 1860.[30] This kind of career-oriented education appealed particularly to city residents because cities housed so many of the institutions requiring employees with specialized training. Moreover, most proprietary professional schools did not require baccalaureate degrees. In 1890, approximately 41,000 students attended schools of law, medicine, and theology, compared with the 64,000 attending baccalaureate colleges. Less than 10 percent of all students in medical schools and 25 percent of those in theology and law schools held a college degree.[31]

As early as 1765, the University of Pennsylvania introduced medical courses, and its School of Medicine became a major part of the university. In 1825, it enrolled 485 students.[32] Two years later, King's College started a medical school, which closed during the American Revolution and then reopened as the Columbia College Medical School. A separate medical school, the College of Physicians and Surgeons, opened in New York in 1807 and merged with Columbia in 1814. For much of this time the medical school operated at a building on 59th Street across from Roosevelt Hospital, where it did much of its teaching. In 1807, the Maryland College of Medicine opened in Baltimore. In 1812, the state chartered it as the University of Maryland, and in subsequent years it opened schools of law (1816), dentistry (1840), and pharmacy (1841). NYU established its medical school in 1841, and two years later Western Reserve College opened a medical department, also known as Cleveland Medical College.

In 1856, a group of physicians set up a free clinic in Brooklyn to care for poor German immigrants. Two years later, New York State chartered it as the Long Island College Hospital and authorized it to confer medical degrees. In 1843, a private, independent medical school in Chicago, Rush Medical College, began instruction. Forty years later, it created the Chicago College of Dental Surgery. Upon the opening of the University of Chicago in 1892, Rush affiliated with this new research university. On the west coast, Cooper Medical College in San Francisco opened in 1858 and merged with the new Toland Medical College six years later. In 1873, the University of California, founded in 1868, assumed responsibility for this medical college and renamed it the Medical Department of the University of California. Thus began the University of California, San Francisco, which added a dental school in 1881 and a college of pharmacy in 1873.

Of the two land-grant colleges located in cities, only the University of Minnesota provided medical instruction in the nineteenth century. It did so by taking over three private medical schools in 1888. In Ohio, various private medical schools opened and merged between 1846 and 1918, when they joined Ohio State University. Catholic universities did not establish medical schools in cities until the end of the nineteenth century, when Creighton University did so. Georgetown University began medical instruction on its rural campus in 1851 and opened a hospital there in 1898. Milwaukee Medical College began in 1894, a few blocks northeast of the Marquette campus at Tenth and State Street. Marquette took it over in 1907. Medically related professional schools of pharmacy, dentistry, and optometry also developed in the cities.

Law schools developed in a similar way. The University of Pennsylvania started the first university-based law school in 1765, just as it was offering its first courses in medicine. NYU law school opened in 1835, Columbia in 1858, Washington University in St. Louis in 1867, Boston University in 1872, Vanderbilt in 1874, Minnesota in 1888, and Ohio State in 1891. Both city land-grants started law schools: Minnesota in 1888 and Ohio State in 1891. In 1878, the Hastings College of Law joined the medical school as part of the University of California, San Francisco. Independent law schools opened in many nineteenth-century cities, and some suburban universities started or acquired law schools in the central city. In 1859, the old University of Chicago (an institution founded in 1857 and closed in 1886) established the Union College of Law downtown. In 1873, as the university faced growing financial problems, it got Northwestern University, located in Evanston, on Chicago's northern border, to jointly operate Union College of Law. After the university closed, Northwestern took over exclusive responsibility for the law school, eventually renamed the Northwestern University Law School.

Few urban Catholic Universities started law schools in the nineteenth century. Saint Louis University's law school opened in 1843 but closed in 1847. Georgetown University, located on the edge of the town of Georgetown, which was not part of Washington until 1871, opened a law school in 1870 and moved it in 1890 into the center of the city of Washington, a few blocks from the U.S. Capitol. But it would not be until the early twentieth century that a larger number of Catholic institutions started law schools in cities.

Informal programs in the mechanical arts provided working adults in cities with instruction, but not college degrees, until late in the nineteenth century. Industrialist Peter Cooper allocated the bulk of his wealth to the education of adult men and women in applied sciences and architectural drawing and design, as well as photography, telegraphy, typewriting, and shorthand specifically for women. Cooper Union in New York began completely free instruction in 1859. Later in the century, it established a four-year engineering college. Across the East River in Brooklyn, another successful industrialist, Charles Pratt, endowed the Pratt Institute, which opened on Clinton Avenue 1887. Pratt offered instruction in architectural engineering and mechanical drawing, as well as liberal arts courses in history, mathematics, physics, and literature. In Chicago, industrialist Philip Danforth Armour gave $1 million to create the Armour Institute in 1893; it offered professional courses in engineering, chemistry, architecture, and library science. Two years later, funds from the estate of hardware merchant Allen C. Lewis launched the Lewis Institute on Chicago's west side, teaching science, engineering, and the liberal arts. In 1940, Armour and Lewis merged to form the Illinois Institute of Technology.

In short, the nineteenth-century collegiate ideal, with its negative view of urban life for college students, restricted the growth of traditional colleges in cities and strongly encouraged those that were in cities to relocate to the periphery and build discrete walled campuses. In contrast, the founders and leaders of professional schools clearly viewed the city as an asset in preparing students for their chosen careers. The continuing industrialization and urbanization of the United States significantly altered this picture in the first half of the twentieth century. Over time, undergraduate liberal education and education for careers became increasingly intertwined. As more and more people started attending college, an ever-increasing proportion of them would do so in urban areas. Undergraduate colleges in twentieth-century cities would soon have to address this radical new reality. How they did so over time would shape contemporary American higher education.

2

Urban Reality, 1900–1945

In the first half of the twentieth century, higher education enrollment grew dramatically, partly as a result of the great expansion of public secondary schools. In 1900, colleges and universities enrolled 237,592 students and conferred 28,691 baccalaureate degrees. By 1940, enrollment had grown to 1,494,203, and institutions conferred 186,500 degrees. The number of colleges and universities also expanded dramatically. Much of this growth, both in undergraduate and professional programs, occurred at institutions in cities. A survey by the US Commissioner of Education reported that in 1924 only 145 of 913 higher education institutions in the United States operated in cities of 100,000 or more. These institutions taught 270,000 of the 664,226 students enrolled that year in all US higher education institutions. A 1928 study listed 150 "schools of collegiate rank" in cities with populations of 100,000 or more. An ever-increasing number of city students lived at home and commuted to college. New York, the nation's largest city, had fifteen colleges. Chicago and Philadelphia, the second- and third-largest, each had six colleges.[1]

This growth of college enrollment in cities in the first three decades of the twentieth century resulted from continuing urban growth, as well as from a substantial increase in those who sought higher education to advance their economic opportunities. The share of the US population living in jurisdictions of 2,500 or more grew from 39.6 percent in 1900 to 56.5 percent in 1940. By 1920, 5.6 million people lived in New York, 2.7 million in Chicago, 1.8 million in Philadelphia, and a little under a million in Detroit. Cleveland, St. Louis, Boston, and Baltimore had populations well over 700,000. On the West Coast, San Francisco and Los Angeles both were home to over a half million people. This growth produced a huge increase in densely populated areas of large cities occupied by low-income people, particularly immigrants. The 1910 census identified 11,826,000 new city residents since 1900. Of these, 41 percent came from abroad.[2]

The growth of large cities caused a wide range of concerns among the nation's elites. Many continued to believe that city growth undermined America's historical foundation and its character. Others focused on the practical issues of how to provide the extensive services and regulation that now seemed essential in dense cities. To do so required a vastly expanded role for government, which many thought ran counter to the American tradition of individualism.[3] Different social reform movements emerged in cities during the Progressive Era to address poverty, housing, health, education, social welfare, and Americanization, among other issues. Given the need to address the social problems facing cities, reformers expressed ever-greater concern about corrupt political machines that controlled many city governments.

By the early twentieth century, most writers, reformers, and civic officials recognized that cities had become integral to American society and vital to its economy. They looked for ways to mitigate the city's worst problems, and in particular to address the negative effects of concentrated population by decentralizing urban areas. A City Beautiful movement encouraged systematic urban planning to reduce population density. In 1910, New York mayor William Jay Garland appointed a Commission on the Congestion of Population. Its report, released the following year, called for creation of more parks and recreational areas, land use regulation, restricting tenement building heights, and regulating the maximum occupancy of residential units. New York and many other cities developed comprehensive city plans to control density and land use. In 1923, urban planners formed the Regional Planning Association of America to support urban decentralization and in particular to advance "garden cities" with large countrified areas.[4]

The reform programs of the New Deal also sought to reduce urban population density. Rexford Tugwell, a key adviser to President Franklin Roosevelt and the head of FDR's Resettlement Administration (RA), explained that he sought "to go just outside centers of population, pick up cheap land, build a whole community and entice people into it." Then government should go "back to the city and tear down whole slums and make parks of them." The RA constructed three "Greenbelt towns" on the edge of Washington, DC, Cincinnati, and Milwaukee.[5] FDR also created the Public Works Administration (PWA) in 1933 to provide federal funding for construction of public facilities, in order to create badly needed jobs. The PWA established a Housing Division, which financed demolition of deteriorated housing and construction of new low-income housing. In 1942, President Roosevelt created the National Housing Agency to expand the federal role in slum clearance and housing construction.[6]

In short, the efforts of Progressive Era and New Deal reformers to address the problems of dense cities reinforced the nation's longstanding commitment to green space. These reform efforts also extended the nation's skepticism about cities. Recognizing that cities served critical economic functions, writers, reformers, and urban planners now sought to decentralize cities rather than simply to restrict their growth. This perspective on cities, like that of nineteenth-century America, deeply influenced American higher education and in particular the growth of universities in urban locations. And the growth of urban higher educational institutions began the process by which urbanization transformed all of American higher education.

Given this urban growth, it is not surprising that many new colleges and universities opened in major cities between 1900 and 1941. Several cities established new municipal colleges or took over existing private institutions. For example, in 1913, the city of Akron took over the financially struggling Buchtel College, founded in 1872 by members of the Universalist Church, renaming it the University of Akron. The Municipal University of Wichita opened in 1926 after the city government purchased Fairmount College, which had provided undergraduate education in the city since 1895. The city of Omaha purchased and took over management of the private Omaha University in 1938. In 1923, Michigan's state legislature established the College of the City of Detroit, an expansion of the two-year Detroit Junior College started six years earlier. In 1933, the city's board of education merged it with city-run schools of medicine, pharmacy, law, and education to create the Colleges of the City of Detroit. The following year, the board changed the institution's name to Wayne University.

Jesuits also opened additional colleges in cities, like Loyola Marymount in Los Angeles in 1911 and Loyola New Orleans in 1912. Rice University opened in Houston, Texas in 1912 as a result of a major bequest, one of a few new private institutions opened in major cities in this period. In Norfolk, Virginia, the state took over a branch of Virginia Union College for black students in 1944, renaming it Norfolk State College.

The city of Newark, New Jersey, the nation's fourteenth largest city in 1910, faced a somewhat unique situation in that it did not have a university. One advocate for Newark higher education complained that "there is no city anywhere in the United States with a population equal to that of Newark which does not have and has not had for many years at least one university and in some cases several."[7] A for-profit law school opened in 1908, a business school in 1929, and an undergraduate liberal arts college in 1930. In 1933, Rutgers University in New Brunswick considered purchasing the various Newark colleges, thereby preventing the possible emergence of a university in Newark that might compete with Rutgers for state funding, but it decided against it because of concerns about the operating costs.[8] The three colleges and two other private institutions merged in 1935 to create the University of Newark, which received no government funding and struggled financially until after World War II.

Very few of those who created colleges for African Americans in the South located them in cities. In 1947, however, the state of Texas took Houston Colored Junior College and Houston College for Negroes and merged them to create Texas Southern University for Negroes. The school's first catalogue described the special advantages of its location in Houston, including the option of attending 250 different Negro churches in the city, art museums, zoological gardens, and the opportunity to study social issues in "a vast human laboratory."[9]

Despite this growth, many educators still insisted that undergraduate students should not attend college in cities, whose populations consisted of ever-greater numbers of immigrants and industrial workers. In 1914, Arthur Lefevre, a school superintendent and college trustee, wrote a report on the needs of Texas higher educational institutions. He extolled "the beauty of university buildings, of their site and of the grounds about them" as a key element in college education. Urban universities, he said, "whose buildings are situated in compactly built streets can never exert on their students all the beneficial influences which suburban or rural universities can exert."[10] Six years later, Colgate University president George Barton Cutten wrote in the *New York Times* that rural colleges encouraged extensive interaction among students and faculty because students lived on campus; moreover, they encouraged much greater attention to academic work because they had none of the distractions that pulled students in cities away from their studies.[11] The president of the University of Akron, George Zook, complained that "the practice of locating colleges, like

Gould Memorial Library, NYU Heights Campus, 1915. Photographer thought to be N. L. Stebbins. Courtesy of New York University.

the practice of locating monasteries, was to put them where the people were *not* rather than where they were."[12]

In 1932, John Huston Finley, former president of City College of New York and New York State commissioner of education, wrote in *The Journal of Higher Education* that "a college or university in the midst of a city cannot do for its students what might be done for them in a place apart, where speech, thought, and manners are under the monopolizing influence of a separate community of tradition, habit and association."[13] That same year, the dean of New York University's residential campus at University Heights in the Bronx proclaimed the virtue of this nonurban NYU campus as "a retired hilltop" a "secluded" place that "shut out the city."[14]

Some educators disagreed sharply with this view. R. H. Eckelberry, a faculty member at Ohio State University, wrote that municipal universities advanced democracy by contributing to "the equalization of educational opportunity." The largest part of the cost of college education, he argued, was "not tuition and fees but living expenses." He hailed the fact that "the city boy who attends his own city college can not only live at home during his college career, but if necessary he can support himself partially or wholly" and noted that all municipal universities conduct night classes.[15] Parke Kolbe, president of the University of Akron, who established the nation's first cooperative education program, argued that in addition to free tuition and the savings from living at home, "a cooperative engineering student, who earns apprentice wages" during those weeks in which he works and does not attend classes, "can secure an education and secure himself at the same time.[16] Some leaders of colleges not municipally funded also recognized the need to educate commuter and adult students.

The Association of Urban Universities

The substantial growth of colleges and universities in cities, and in particular the expansion of the number of commuter students in the early twentieth century, raised a wide range of questions for the leaders of these institutions. Given the rural-residential tradition of American undergraduate education, they had to determine how to address the collegiate ideal with a student body consisting largely or entirely of commuters. They had to decide what it meant to be an urban university and how to build on the traditional strengths of professional education programs in cities. They needed to determine how to use the resources of the city to advance instruction and research. And they had to evaluate what responsibilities, if any, they had to their host cities.

In 1914, the presidents of two municipal universities, Charles Dabney of the University of Cincinnati and Parke Kolbe of the University of Akron, organized the first meeting of the Association of Urban Universities (AUU) to give presidents and other senior leaders of universities in cities an opportunity to share experiences and to consider the role of universities in relation to the communities in which they were located. Dabney had begun serving as president of the University of Cincinnati ten years before creating the AUU. Kolbe had taught modern language at Buchtel College. In 1913, after the city of Akron took over the college and renamed it the Municipal University of Akron, Kolbe was appointed its president. In 1925 the trustees of the Polytechnic Institute of Brooklyn appointed him president, and in 1932 he joined Drexel Institute in Philadelphia as president. In 1928, he published *Urban Influences on Higher Education in England and the United States*, one of the very first books about urban universities.

University of Cincinnati, c. 1910–1920. Courtesy of the Library of Congress Prints & Photographs Online Catalog (digital ID det 4a25665).

Dabney originally planned to include only municipal colleges and universities but then decided that all universities located in cities should be invited to join the association. The initial membership included all of the municipal universities (Akron, City College, Hunter, Cincinnati, Louisville, and Toledo). Private institutions included Johns Hopkins University, Washington University in St. Louis, NYU, the University of Pittsburgh, Boston University, the University of Buffalo, Temple, the University of Pennsylvania, and Northwestern.[17] The founding institutions also included nondenominational Reed College in Portland, Oregon, which had opened just three years earlier, and Presbyterian-affiliated Millikin University in Decatur, Illinois, founded in 1901. Many other private universities in cities joined the following year, including Brown, Case, Clark, Drexel, Chicago, Syracuse, Rochester, Vanderbilt, Harvard, and Western Reserve. The two city land-grants, Minnesota and Ohio

State, also joined that year, along with the University of Washington (in Seattle) and two smaller state universities, the University of Tennessee in Knoxville and the University of Vermont in Burlington. The University of Toronto also joined. Columbia University did not join until 1939.

It is interesting that no Catholic Universities joined the AUU until 1929, when Fordham became a member. Detroit University joined in 1931, St. John's and Loyola New Orleans in 1939. Church leaders located the vast majority of Catholic universities in cities. The Jesuits, who established about half of these colleges, typically gave them the name of their home city, including Baltimore, Boston, Buffalo, Chicago, Cincinnati, Cleveland, Detroit, Manhattan, New Orleans, and San Francisco. They chose city locations largely because the Catholic population of the United States grew rapidly in the nineteenth and early twentieth centuries due to immigration of Catholics from places like Germany, Ireland, Italy, Poland, and Mexico, most of whom settled in cities.

The leaders of Catholic colleges, however, did not share the concerns articulated by many others in higher education regarding commuter students and the challenges of cities. However some did share the view that their campuses should be located on the outskirts of the city and not in downtown. The first catalogue of St. Francis College, opened in Brooklyn in 1884, stated that "the college is situated in a healthy and retired part of the city."[18] Certainly, Catholic colleges in cities sought ways to adapt the education they offered to their urban environment.

The term "urban university" had rarely been used before the founding of the AUU. The first article in the *New York Times* using this term appeared in 1913, in an article written by an NYU journalism professor comparing students in a rural college who worked to cover the cost of their education with students who did so in an urban university.[19] The term did not appear again in the *Times* until the 1920s, when it was used seven times. The first use of the term "urban college" appeared in 1928, in an article describing the upcoming AUU meeting in New York, and in a second article a month later.[20] In the 1930s, "urban university" appeared nineteen times and "urban college" six times.

The leaders of institutions that joined the AUU in the years after 1914 agreed that a city location in and of itself was insufficient to define an urban university. Some argued that urban universities had to teach about and study cities and to engage students in the city as part of their education. Others insisted that urban universities had to build close ties with local communities.

Some even insisted that they take the lead in solving the growing problems of cities. In addition, some argued that an urban university also had to have a majority of its students living in the institution's home city.

At the first AUU meeting, in 1914, Charles Dabney asserted that municipal universities existed, in part, to provide education to poor and working-class students who otherwise could not afford to go to college. "The municipal university is the one thing needed to complete our American system of higher education," he claimed. He touted the importance of extension programs offered by colleges in cities and talked about the many resources a city had to offer—libraries, museums, art galleries, hospitals, social and political institutions, industrial laboratories, and commercial establishments.[21] Dabney and many others also argued that cities offered the ideal location for a liberal arts college because students could combine traditional academic study with hands-on experience.

Under Dabney, the University of Cincinnati established the first cooperative education program in the country, in 1904, in which students in professional programs like engineering, medicine, and teacher preparation split their time between classroom work and paid work in factories, medical facilities, schools, and businesses. Since a large number of rubber plants clustered in Akron, the university created a fully equipped laboratory and specialized program for the study of the chemistry of rubber. The engineering college offered a program in which students alternated in two-week periods between class at the campus and work in one of nearly a dozen local rubber factories. The university also developed a cooperative course for juniors studying medicine in which they spent some of their time working with the city's board of health.[22]

In a similar vein, the writer of an article on how municipal universities cooperated with city governments reported in 1916 that CCNY's chemistry department had students working "in direct cooperation with the city's laboratories" and that University of Toledo baccalaureate students had to do eighteen hours a week of work in the city relevant to their major and also do "a constructive piece of work for the municipality" or "complete a task . . . of interest and value to the citizens of Toledo."[23] And the dean of NYU's undergraduate Washington Square College wrote that "today, the most impressive feature of American education is the rise of the American urban university," which "uses the life of the city as its laboratory" and coordinates liberal arts and professional education "to obtain a more efficient and perhaps a more practical education."[24]

NYU Washington Square East campus. Date unknown. Photographer thought to be Henry J. Sihler. Courtesy of New York University.

The *National Municipal Review* in 1916 reported enthusiastically on the second annual meeting of the AAU, stating that "the primarily urban university is very naturally placing first emphasis on city problems."[25] A. Monroe Stowe, president of the University of the City of Toledo, in 1927 wrote that the aim of his institution, and the proper aim of other city universities, should be to develop "efficient citizens, alive to the social, economic and civic problems which spring from the exceedingly complex life of our modern cities [and] capable of contributing their share to the practical solutions of such problems."[26] Just before the start of World War II, NYU chancellor Harry Woodburn Chase told AUU attendees that the term "urban university" does not necessarily mean a university located in a city. "Definition is not a matter of geography," he explained. Rather, he defined an urban university as an institution "which finds its prime field of service in the community in which it is located."[27] A senior administrator of Marquette University in Milwaukee, Edward A. Fitzpatrick, in that same year wrote that universities must "send men into the city to whom public service—social service—human service—is felt to be an inescapable personal responsibility."[28]

Defining the Needs of Urban Students

To be recognized as an urban university did the institution also need to enroll large numbers of local residents? The vast majority of students at municipal universities, of course, lived in the city. According to a report, published in 1937 by the US Office of Education, "The term urban university in this country generally refers to a classification of institutions of higher learning that are located in cities and are dependent for their student body to a greater or less [*sic*] degree on their local communities"; such universities also enrolled a substantial number of adults.[29]

The problems and needs of urban students quickly emerged as one of the main points of discussion at the AUU's annual conferences. Conference attendees expressed deep concern about the social class and ethnic backgrounds of city students. Charles Fay, dean of Tufts College, explained in 1917 that his institution had once been rural but now drew most of its students from Boston and other nearby cities. Although the students who came to Tufts "in the early days," he said, "came from rustic families," they "had a background and ideals very different from those of the students who come to us today." Current students, he observed, come from the lower classes. "They are naturally people without background," and "they lack . . . imagination." Therefore, although "they can apprehend a fact perfectly well," they "have had nothing at home, and I fear very little in the schools, to prepare them for actual literary work."[30]

Kenneth Mason, dean of freshmen at Brown University, worried that his institution, "in common with other institutions located in a like environment, has in her student body too large a proportion of socially undesirable students." Emphatically denying that he was "Jew-baiting," he expressed grave concern about "the influx of alien blood into what was not so long ago a homogeneous group of students prevailingly Baptist and Anglo-Saxon." The social background and breeding of many students, he continued, "are such as to make their college training of little value to society." On a more upbeat note, Frank McCloskey, assistant dean at NYU, reported that the homes where his students "have been reared and in which they still live, inevitably retain the old world customs, the old world atmosphere—frequently even the old world language," despite parents' efforts to encourage their children's assimilation to American culture. Given these home influences, students' "observable achievements during a four-year college course are often astounding."[31]

Higher education leaders articulated this concern over students' backgrounds in publications and forums other than those of the AUU. For example, in a 1916 *Harper's Monthly* article entitled "Should Students Study?" the president of Reed College reasoned that "one might conclude, from the studiousness of the boys at the College of the City of New York, that large, free urban universities are the usual resorts of serious-minded youth . . . [but] such a conclusion would ignore the racial factor, more important in this instance than any other."[32]

NYU Heights campus dean Archibald Louis Bouton, in a 1919 speech, asserted that because of the country's unrestricted immigration policy, "the sons of unassimilated or partially assimilated immigrants are now filling our urban universities." Bouton complained that these students "segregate themselves" on campus exactly as in the city outside." Selective admissions provided the solution for this problem at the NYU Heights campus. It would enable the university to "modify the composition of the student body" so that "Americanizing influences" would shape students' experience. NYU's chancellor, Elmer Ellsworth Brown, defended selective admissions arguing that "the influx of Jews [had to] be checked" because the "cultural background" of these children of immigrants "was dismally un-American."[33]

Although most private universities in cities sought to control enrollment of students from immigrant families, officials at many municipal colleges and state universities could not significantly restrict enrollment. So they had to address this concern about students' backgrounds through academic and extracurricular activities. Hunter College president George Samler Davis, in his address at the graduation of the class of 1923, expressed enthusiasm for the role of this women's college in Americanizing its students who then brought American values and culture learned in college to their neighborhoods.[34] His successor, Eugene Colligan, made providing "social and moral guidance" to students a central goal of Hunter education.[35] In the 1930s, Hunter College dean Hannah Egan set up a program of compulsory "Dean's Hour Courses" to teach students proper attire, personal appearance, hygiene, behavior, and, in the words of the dean, "to be at ease, serving, conversing, meeting people." In his autobiography, George Shuster, who became president of Hunter in 1939, explained that when he assumed the leadership of the college, "a large number of the girls who came to Hunter had absorbed a variety of prejudices from home environments, displayed only the rudiments of good manners, spoke English atrociously, and had as little use for honor societies as they did for Herbert

Hoover." He described these students, mostly the daughters of Jewish immigrants, as "raucous, gawky, and afflicted with acne, halitosis, and deplorable hair-dos." The faculty, he reported, asserted that Hunter must teach students to "become socially and morally the kind of women who are deserving of a Hunter degree. This meant teaching them "a sense of honor and public service" and inculcating "charm and courtesy."[36]

New York City's Board of Higher Education actually attempted in 1938 to ban alien residents, largely refugees from Europe who had not yet obtained citizenship, from attending the city's municipal colleges. About six months later, after considerable protest, the board reversed its decision for applicants intending to become American citizens.[37]

Faculty and administrators at the private University of Newark expressed similar views. A 1937 study found that first- and second-generation Americans constituted more than half of the student body and nearly half of students enrolled lived in Newark; 43 percent identified their religion as Jewish, 28 percent as Protestant, and 25 percent as Catholic. The director of student relations in 1938 described the faculty and staff's relationship with students as "unpredictable" because "we do not adequately appreciate the various influences brought to bear upon their lives outside the realm of the University's influence." She went on to explain that the university had the responsibility of teaching students "the abc's of social relationships."[38]

Some higher educators extended this call for character development to include emphasis on religious values. In 1939, Ordway Tead, chair of the New York City Board of Higher Education addressed the AUU: "The process of secularization has proceeded, certainly in urban institutions," to a point that is "beyond all reason, sense and public benefit." Tead called for emphasis on spiritual training to correct an "overemphasis on intellectualist training."[39]

As late as 1944, a report prepared for a New York State legislative committee regarding New York City's publicly supported colleges noted that only 17 percent of the fathers and 22 percent of the mothers of freshmen who entered City College were born in the United States, concluding that "City College students must often be torn between European and American standards, between the codes and customs of their parents and those of their own group." The report also indicated that many had grown up in low-income homes where there had been "a continuous and severe struggle for existence." Noting that three-quarters of the students held outside employment while attending college, it stated that as a result many students "were poorly adjusted." Personnel counselors reported a higher "incidence of acute personality problems" among students from immigrant families as compared to other student populations.[40]

One largely commuter institution, the University of Pittsburgh, took unusual steps to address what faculty saw as the deficiencies of students from immigrant backgrounds, who attended the university in large numbers. In his annual report to the trustees in 1926, Chancellor John Bowman wrote that some students came "from localities which hold to the language and traditions of another country," thereby limiting their capacity "to get the viewpoint and attitude which make up our national traditions." The university sought, he continued, "through a thorough education, to assimilate such students, but starting as we do from our own Anglo-Saxon character, we find difficulty in arriving quite upon common ground with students of other inheritance." Many faculty shared this view. A modern language professor, for example, said the problem of educating students from immigrant families was "not with the training of the mind, but in social refinement."[41]

After World War I, the university took an unusual approach in addressing this problem. It decided to create sixteen nationality rooms in a major new building, each one containing artifacts and artwork from a country with a large immigrant population in Pittsburgh. Bowman believed that this would help him raise money for the new structure from the more prosperous members of immigrant communities and facilitate the assimilation of students of foreign ancestry. In 1942, Bowman declared that the completed rooms had exceeded all expectations. "They make for good will and good manners."[42]

Even as higher education leaders expressed unease about the character deficiencies of local students from immigrant families, they also articulated concerns about the influence of the urban environment itself on students from both immigrant and nonimmigrant families. At the 1920 AAU annual meeting, Carl Holliday, College of Arts and Sciences dean at Toledo University, a municipal institution, asserted, "There is no American who needs more sorely the genuine riches of civilization than the city boy." Describing city youth as "flashy" and prone to "superficial . . . brilliancy with no depth," he determined that "the vision of man's place in the universe is perhaps more difficult of placement in the city lad's head than in the cranium of the unsophisticated country boy" because "a thousand non-essentials clamor for the city dweller's attention."[43] In 1928, Parke Kolbe, former president of the University of Akron and now president of the Polytechnic Institute of Brooklyn, wrote that "youth of the college age is particularly susceptible to beauty of surroundings" and

Cathedral of Learning at University of Pittsburgh, completed in 1937. Courtesy of the Library of Congress Prints & Photographs Online Catalog (digital ID thc 5a36301).

that attending college on a campus without it "does definitely injure the development of the aesthetic sense."[44]

Added to the negative perceptions of immigrant working-class families and of the urban environment itself were those regarding the unsuitability of students commuting from home to college. Dean Mason of Brown University reported in his discourse on non–Anglo Saxon urban students that a Brown alumnus complained to him about these "carpet-bagger" students coming to campus only for class, taking "no part in college life and 'giving back nothing of benefit.'"[45]

Although most higher education leaders seldom expressed such open hostility to commuters, they agreed that commuting greatly diminished the ability of colleges to build character and refinement in their students. CCNY president Frederick Robinson, for example, acknowledged in 1928 that commuters "do not enter into a student life dominated night and day by fellow students" and therefore "miss the advantages of spiritual transplanting." Moreover, while away from college "their older associations and habits compete more powerfully with . . . academic influences."[46] In 1933, Clarence Marsh, a dean at the University of Buffalo, complained to his fellow AUU attendees that "when I step outside my door in the hall of an urban institution I see and hear . . . too much boorishness and too little of what is embodied in the word gentility." He pointed out that when he had attended a residential college, students acquired gentility from the other resident students. He proposed that urban institutions "pick out one or two men who . . . have the proper gifts in personality" and have them conduct seminars for all seniors "to discuss the art of living or a philosophy of life."[47]

In 1935, the president of the Association of Urban Universities asked its members for suggestions on how urban commuter students could get more of the college life experiences of traditional resident students. Twenty-four institutions responded. Only three rejected the goal of character development and declared that urban institutions should concern themselves exclusively with student intellectual development. All others agreed that their institutions should find ways to enhance the life of commuters outside the classroom. Several called for a building where nonresident students could gather and socialize with each other, with resident students, and with faculty. Others urged vigorous commitment to organized student activities—student government, fraternities and sororities, intramural athletics, academic clubs, annual banquets, special freshmen orientation, publications, excursions, theater parties, and religious societies. Several also recommended that juniors and seniors be assigned to mentor freshmen.[48] Urban commuter students, they asserted, faced enormous obstacles, but urban colleges still had to build character and refinement in their students as best they could.[49]

Adult Education

If educating working-class, immigrant, and commuter students posed a challenge, the education of adult part-time students in evening programs violated even more the conventional norms in the years before 1945. At an NYU conference in 1911, one speaker praised public lectures and full courses for adults, but another, while agreeing that "earnest and attentive" adult listeners attended these lectures, doubted that they were truly educational because they were "primarily informational."[50] In 1918, Charles Thwing expressed deep skepticism about education programs for "men of mature years." He explained that "many men desiring to become students are found to lack a proper general education." Their enthusiasm to study social issues "cannot be accepted as a substitute for a trained intellect."[51]

Yet despite this skepticism, municipal and other universities serving city populations embraced adult education as a logical extension of their mission and as an added source of tuition revenue. Whereas land-grant universities in rural areas developed extension programs offering instruction at remote locations, urban institutions conducted courses for adults largely in their regular facilities, but often through separate evening colleges or divisions. Many municipal universities developed programs to train public school teachers in after-school courses. Many also developed nondegree courses to improve the quality of work in particular industries. For example, the University of Louisville cooperated with the local chapter of the American Institute of Architects in offering courses on architectural design and history for men employed by local architectural firms so they could become "more than draughtsmen." Likewise, it offered night courses for hospital employees in physiology, hygiene, and bacteriology and for charity and social service workers in "theoretical and practical sociology."[52]

Catholic universities developed the same kinds of night classes to serve adults. In 1896, Xavier University began evening lectures for Cincinnati residents. The University of Detroit started "extension lectures" in 1909 and an evening school in 1912. In 1913, Boston College established an evening college offering master's degrees but terminated it a year later because faculty did not want to teach graduate students at night.[53]

By the late 1920s, evening programs enrolled approximately 100,000 students. Attendees of the AUU annual meetings discussed adult and evening students extensively. In 1935, leaders of evening colleges and adult education programs, who had been attending the AUU meetings regularly, formed a separate Association of Deans and Directors of Evening Colleges. This new organization remained closely aligned with the AUU.[54]

But even as attendees at AUU meetings extolled the virtues of adult education, they frequently pointed to the severe social problems in the cities from which their students came. Echoing their colleagues who maintained that college education should promote character development in traditional-aged students, they argued that education of adult and evening students would help to mitigate urban problems by enhancing these students' civic responsibility. In 1930, the AUU passed a resolution lauding "the importance of a program of adult education to American welfare, especially in the great population centers." The resolutions committee, in presenting its proposal, explained that "the social and law enforcement problems of the community are minimized by the education of the adult, even though the courses of instruction bear no relation to these problems themselves."[55]

"Doubt lingers in the minds of some . . . as to how far a university should go, if at all, in extending its off-campus service to adults," University of Minnesota president Lotus Coffman told attendees at an NYU-sponsored conference titled "The Obligations of Universities to the Social Order" two years later. "There are those who look upon this practice as prostitution of learning, and others who look upon it as a sheer and unmitigated dissipation of the intellectual life." Nonetheless, state universities, he declared, have taken on this responsibility "with all the effectiveness at their command."[56] And in 1941, the president of the Association of Deans and Directors of University Evening Schools passionately defended the need to educate adult students in cities:

> Whether our cities become deep and deeper cesspools of degradation, misery, radicalism, and crime, or grow into centers of light, learning, and leadership for the nation, depends not upon any further increase in productive and managerial capacity, as valuable as that might be, but upon whether we help our adults to develop more open, tolerant, thoughtful minds; to enrich their lives and refine their tastes for those things that distinguish us from the brutes; and to build up those wise social and civic ideals which alone make civilization possible and life worth living. . . . [N]othing but better adult education can save civilization from a complete collapse.[57]

In the same spirit, the University of Newark planned a continuing adult education program in five communities to examine the "origin, growth, and development of prejudice" and "how it can be constructively combatted."[58]

Several scholars even undertook research to determine if adult students could learn as well as students of traditional college age, mostly concluding that they performed as well as the younger students in day programs.[59] Despite this research, college faculty and administrators expressed concern about the negative influences of cities on adult students.

Some leaders of urban universities offered an affirmative defense of their commuter students. A professor of English at the University of Cincinnati proclaimed that "in an urban university, you teach children who come from all classes—children of day laborers, policemen, the white collar group, the well-to-do, the mature men and women seeking to supplement their private reading." If the urban university, he continued, "is less suited to afford to the undergraduate what is called college life, that is the life of a more intelligent country club, it is better suited to turn out lawyers, physicians, engineers, and teachers."[60] In 1920, a study of working students at the Municipal University of Akron found that they displayed high levels of initiative, perseverance, self-confidence, and reliability. These students had also "come into more direct contact with the life of the business world than most college students" and therefore had learned "how to mix with men of all classes" and "how to handle men to gain his desires."[61]

Defenders of working-class, immigrant, adult, and commuter students touted the educational opportunities of the city to mitigate, at least partially, the prevailing view that these students lacked the personal qualities of those who experienced traditional campus life. Yet in doing so, they reinforced the definition of urban university as an institution enrolling working class, immigrant, and adult commuter students.

Addressing the Needs of City Government

As cities grew rapidly, various organizations emerged to foster greater effectiveness in the ever more complex responsibilities of municipal governments, often dominated by local political machines. Citizens joined together to create local improvement associations aimed at expanding municipal services and promoting capital projects. These associations began to unite to form citywide municipal leagues. Philadelphia's league in 1896 organized a national conference of municipal leagues devoted to "good city government," resulting in the founding of the National Municipal League. As the weaknesses of city governments continued despite the efforts of these organizations, Progressive Era urban reformers began to recognize that improvement required systematic research on the city and its government.

In 1906, reformers in New York City established a Bureau of City Betterment to improve efficiency, to promote the use of scientific accounting methods, and to "collect, to classify, to analyze, to correlate, to interpret and to publish facts as to the administration of municipal government." The office soon changed its name to the Bureau of Municipal Research. It raised a good deal of money and within six years its staff grew from two to almost fifty people. Other cities followed suit: Philadelphia in 1908, Cincinnati in 1909, Chicago in 1910, and Milwaukee in 1913. By 1926, bureaus of municipal research functioned in more than forty cities. Some bureaus created training schools for public servants. The first of these, in New York, opened in 1907.[62]

These organizations did not initially engage universities in this municipal research. However, many scholars in some of the new academic disciplines created in the late nineteenth century expressed keen interest in local urban research. University of Chicago political scientist Charles Merriam, for example, who served on the Chicago City Council and ran unsuccessfully for mayor, had deep interest in applied research on the city. A committee of the American Political Science Association (APSA), founded in 1903, urged the profession in 1908 to improve the training of city government employees. In 1911, the APSA's committee on instruction called on political scientists to prepare government administrators and to train lawyers, journalists and other professionals to understand city government. The American Economics Society joined the APSA in advocating professional training for city workers.

The APSA then launched a journal, the *Public Servant*, and set up its ongoing Committee on Practical Training. Edward Fitzpatrick, who edited the journal and served as executive secretary of the committee, wrote in 1914 in the *American Political Science Review* that "nowhere in the United States is there a training school for public service," even though many universities had established programs for other professions, including physicians, lawyers, engineers, and farmers. Elsewhere he declared that "Public Service is not a profession," and therefore public administration "is in the hands of amateurs." The committee prepared a list of places "where laboratory work for graduate students in political science can be done." It also urged universities to develop a plan whereby doctoral candidates could spend a year in public agencies under academic supervision.[63] Columbia University political scientist and historian Charles Beard strongly endorsed the call for university training in public administration, arguing that good education required both "knowing" and "doing," and complained of the poor quality of the literature on civil service reform.[64]

The National Municipal League showed considerable interest in developing professional education for city administrators. In 1900, it created a committee chaired by the president of Lehigh University to report on municipal government instruction at American colleges and universities. A second committee, chaired by Harvard political scientist William Bennett Munro, reported in 1913 that sixty-four institutions offered instruction on municipal government, eighteen more than five years before. It also reported that fifty-five of these colleges and universities provided students with "opportunities for some sort of actual contact with the practical problems of municipal administration." In 1915, the league created a committee to collaborate with the APSA and the AEA in efforts to promote education for municipal workers.[65]

Meanwhile, leaders of municipal research bureaus argued vigorously for systematic education of city employees. In 1911, donors gave the New York Bureau of Municipal Research $120,000 to train "the men who, throughout the country, will aid in the work of applying the tests of scientific management to municipal business."[66] Three years later, the director of the Texas Bureau of Municipal Research and Reference asked rhetorically, "How can our universities with a clear conscience emphasize the importance of getting expert administrators in the city's service when they do nothing to train such experts?" He then called for the creation of separate departments of municipal administration in universities.[67] And the Association of Urban Universities devoted the bulk of its 1915 conference to discussion of university training for public service. It returned to the subject after American entry into World War I.

Nonetheless, only a few universities responded to the call for teaching and research on municipal administration. The University of California's extension division established a Bureau of Municipal Reference for use by officials of California municipalities, using the resources of the university to improve government quality.[68] NYU created a municipal information bureau to provide citizens with data about the city government and New York City's problems.[69] The University of Michigan began a master's degree in municipal administration in 1914, which included six months of work with the Detroit Bureau of Governmental Research. Charles Beard got Columbia University to consider establishing a public administration program, but senior university officials decided against it because they believed enrollment would be small.

After World War I, more universities, mostly in urban areas, established programs in public administration. A political scientist at Ohio State University told the 1917 AUU attendees that the war highlighted the need not only for professionally trained military officials but also for municipal administrators who had to deal with the greatly increased wartime demands on city governments.[70] In 1918, Akron University president Parke Kolbe announced that graduate students would be placed in the city's departments of engineering, charity, health, and research.[71] In the early 1920s, programs in public administration began at the University of Wisconsin, Stanford, Texas A&M, Toledo University, William & Mary, and the University of California, Berkeley. Philanthropist George Maxwell endowed a major public administration program at Syracuse University in 1924.[72]

Universities in cities also worked closely with another major branch of city government, the public schools. They collaborated with public school systems to provide in-service training for teachers and to prepare new and more highly qualified teachers. Many of them established schools of education to meet this need, especially as school systems and states elevated education requirements for teachers. NYU opened the first of these, the School of Pedagogy, in 1890. By 1900, the school enrolled more than 200 students, and it grew to over 550 by 1915. However, NYU's school did not seek to duplicate the work of the normal schools, which typically did not offer a full four-year baccalaureate program. It enrolled college graduates in a master's and a doctoral program to prepare graduates for positions as school principals and superintendents. And it recruited graduates of normal schools and others who had attended college for two or three years to its baccalaureate program to prepare classroom teachers.[73]

Shortly after he began his tenure as president at the University of Cincinnati, Charles Dabney developed with the city public school superintendent a Teachers College jointly funded and managed by the university and the school system. The college offered baccalaureate education for new teachers and also provided late afternoon courses for classroom teachers with more limited training. By 1920, the college had trained 800 of the public schools' 1,100 teachers. It also examined applicants for teacher positions, recommended instructors for promotion, and held courses that, upon completion, gave the enrollees salary increases.[74] Although Dabney's collaboration proved uniquely successful, most other municipal universities also worked closely with the public schools. So did Catholic universities, preparing teachers for both public and Catholic parochial schools, and some private universities like NYU.

Other Community Service Activities

In addition to using city institutions for fieldwork and other kinds of experiential teaching, for research, and for the development of municipal administration, universities in cities engaged in a wide range of other activities they defined as serving the community. Such activities proliferated at the new urban research universities founded in the late nineteenth century. They worked with city school systems to upgrade teacher preparation and to restructure public school governance in ways that would limit machine politicians' power over the hiring of teachers and principals and over other aspects of school management. They used insights from current research in psychology, sociology, political science, social work, law, statistics, and other fields to advocate major changes in the criminal justice system and in the treatment of juvenile delinquents. Several universities established social settlements to enable students and faculty to learn about low-income workers, immigrants, and African Americans. Some faculty advocated unionization of industrial workers, higher salaries, and health and safety laws for manufacturers. And several sought to advance the arts. Brown University, for example, created a Community Art Project in 1939, arranging large and small art exhibitions, community lectures on art, and demonstrations of block printing.[75]

Municipal universities expressed the greatest passion for service to their cities, although their research and graduate programs were not nearly as extensive as those at private research universities. In 1908, Charles Dabney wrote that while a state land-grant university like Wisconsin could provide a range of services to agriculture, industry, and state government, the municipal university, because of its close relationship to its constituency, "can perform many kinds of public service impracticable for State and much more for private institutions." He explained that "the university of the city, as distinguished from the university in the city," should be the city's brain, directing the goals and policies of all its entities and its residents. Once cities recognize this, "boundless possibilities for service appear." Four years later, he told educators attending a meeting of the National Education Association that since "city problems are still the greatest problem of democracy, where, if not to its own university, shall the city turn for help in the solution?"[76] In that same year, Charles Levermore, president of Adelphi College, complained that universities did not give the needs of their cities high priority. He proposed "a university amply endowed and situated in each one of the great cities of our country that is not yet provided with such a powerhouse for souls." These municipal universities would become "the matrix of all the higher directive educational forces and processes for a great urban community and its suburban dependencies."[77]

Some Catholic universities echoed this commitment to their host cities. An 1897 editorial in *The Catholic World* hailed the opening of Trinity College because Washington, DC, offered extraordinary opportunities for students, among them "the libraries and museums, as well as many of the educational institutes and the scientific collections."[78] On Marquette University's twenty-fifth anniversary, in 1906, when it was relatively small but on the verge of acquiring local law and medical schools and establishing its Department of Science and Engineering and School of Business Administration, the archbishop declared that "what a state university does for Madison, a university located here would do for Milwaukee." Albert Fox, Marquette president from 1922 to 1928, promoted the institution as "Milwaukee's University." In an essay entitled "University's Vision of a City," he argued that a first-rate university needed an extensive civic partnership with its home city. And by 1924, non-Catholics constituted more than 40 percent of Marquette students.[79]

In the years before and just after the founding of the Association of Urban Universities, few institutions in cities could boast as extensive a range of community activities as Charles Dabney's University of Cincinnati. But they all engaged in city-oriented activities of one kind or another. They educated working-class and immigrant day students and adult night students, leading the nation in democratizing higher education. They built ties with local industries and offered courses for their workers. They undertook training and research to meet the needs of city governments and public schools. Although higher education leaders still had considerable ambivalence about urban life and the shortcomings of commuter and immigrant students, they recognized that urbanization would continue and increasingly shape higher education; therefore, they had to address these issues as best they could.

As universities in cities grew and college enrollments expanded, the discussion of higher education's responsibility for educating local residents, working-class people, and minorities emerged as a major concern. So did universities' role in providing research and expertise for government, industry, and public schools; engaging students in hands-on learning; and many other issues. In the second half of the twentieth century, urban universities' perspective on these matters would significantly influence all of American higher education.

3

Postwar Higher Education and the Needs of Cities, 1945–1963

In the years following the end of World War II, colleges and universities in cities continued to lead America's democratization of higher education by extending baccalaureate education to ever-larger numbers of working-class commuters, immigrants, ethnic minorities, and adults. They engaged increasingly in urban research and support of city governments. They expanded their role in addressing urban problems and the needs of their communities, leading to a near consensus by higher education leaders across the country that community service constituted a core university mission (along with teaching and research). Higher education institutions in cities also took greater advantage of opportunities for teaching and learning in city institutions, despite continuing reservations about the influence of cities on young people and the shortcomings of commuting to college. A few private city universities also worked with their municipal governments to upgrade campus neighborhoods through urban renewal.

The postwar urban population grew dramatically in suburbs but actually declined in central cities. Between 1950 and 1960, the census reported that the population of suburbs increased by 60 percent, accounting for two-thirds of the nation's total population growth. The populations of Boston, St. Louis, and Pittsburgh declined by more than 10 percent, and those of Detroit, Minneapolis, and Buffalo by 7–10 percent. New York, Chicago, Philadelphia, Cleveland, Baltimore, and Cincinnati also lost population, but at a lower rate.[1] Those leaving the cities for the suburbs had middle-class incomes and typically moved to single-family houses. Low-income people, many of them African Americans from the South, continued to move to cities. Just under 1.5 million black people left the South in the 1940s, and over a million in the 1950s.

The vast majority came to major cities. New York and Chicago received the largest number, followed by Detroit, Philadelphia, St. Louis, and Cleveland. Because of widespread racial discrimination in housing, they had to concentrate in overwhelmingly black "ghetto" neighborhoods.[2]

Politicians, writers, journalists, and others increasingly talked about the deterioration and the social ills of central cities. Many factors contributed to the decline of central city populations. Racism and federal government policies played a key role. The GI Bill, passed in 1944 to assist veterans, provided low-interest loans enabling white veterans to purchase suburban homes. The US Housing Act of 1949 supplied federal funds for "urban redevelopment," consisting of slum clearance and construction of public housing in central cities, as well as increased financing for housing purchases. Slum clearance displaced large numbers of residents. By the end of the 1950s, nonwhites made up nearly nine of every ten families forced to move. Government officials who selected sites for public housing projects did so in ways that reinforced racial segregation. Many white residents fled the city when black people moved to areas adjacent to their neighborhoods, often using low-interest federal loans to purchase homes in all-white suburbs. By 1954, these federal programs came to be known as "urban renewal." By the early 1960s, African American writers and political leaders often asserted that "urban renewal means Negro removal."[3]

Traditional American anti-urbanism also contributed to the decline of central city populations. President John F. Kennedy proposed establishment of a federal cabinet-level department of Urban Affairs and Housing. Southern politicians opposed it because they saw it as a vehicle to help black people. Suburban, small town, and rural legislators opposed it because they thought it would enhance central cities at their expense. A Republican congressman from Nebraska, Glenn Cunningham, fought against the proposed new cabinet department, arguing that small towns were "dying on the vine." He proposed instead that Congress establish a Department of Small Towns and Rural Affairs.[4]

Postsecondary enrollment expanded dramatically in the years after World War II. The GI bill provided tuition to large numbers of veterans, reducing for many the cost of attending college. Increasing numbers of students graduated from high school. In 1940, only 44 percent of American youth graduated from secondary school. By 1960, 62 percent did so, and roughly one-third of nineteen- and twenty-year-olds attended college. US postsecondary enrollment grew from about 1.5 million students in 1939–40 to 3.7 million in 1959–60. US colleges awarded 186,000 baccalaureate degrees in 1940 and 392,000 in 1960.

Since an ever-larger portion of the nation's population lived in urban areas, state and local governments created numerous new institutions in cities and some suburbs to accommodate this demand for higher education.[5] Commuters now constituted more than half of America's college students.

Emergence of the "Urban University"

This dramatic growth of urban commuter enrollment created a sense of urgency among the leaders of urban higher education institutions to define what it meant to be an "urban university" and how the mission of urban institutions could transform both American higher education and American cities.

In 1944, as Wayne University planned for its future in industrial Detroit, it invited architect Joseph Hudnut, dean of design at Harvard, to speak to faculty about Wayne's future potential. "We have in America *urban universities*," he stated, that have "achieved a new dignity" in light of their importance "to the great cities that nurture them." He expressed deep concern that America's large cities "have conferred on man his deepest indignity, making him an automaton," and urged universities in cities to develop "in the minds and hearts of students, whether young or adult . . . such attitudes as will fit them for the collective life of the city."[6]

In a speech celebrating the centennial of the University of Buffalo, Chancellor Samuel Capan, a national leader of the urban university movement, explained that the term "urban university" "designates something other than the mere accident of location." It has a "special obligation" to respond to the educational needs of its community and to be "hospitable to all local requests for those intellectual services which a university may legitimately render."[7] In that same year, American University president Paul Douglass gave a talk to the Association of Urban Universities (AUU), titled "The University in the Urban Age." The ever-more-complex modern city placed great stresses on its residents, he argued, and universities in cities now constituted the primary agency to mediate them. "The urban university cannot build a wall around the stresses of community life," he argued, because "it is the catalytic agent of the 20th-century neighborhood."[8]

At the 1955 meeting of the AUU, University of Illinois president David Henry repeated the familiar refrain that the urban university played a major role in equalizing higher educational opportunity. But he complained that the urban university "is still not recognized adequately in the educational councils of the nation."[9] Four years later, University of Buffalo chancellor C. C. Furniss asked, "Why an urban university?" He answered saying it is responsive to community needs, provides opportunities for low-income students to work while attending college, is "a pipeline to the outside world," and offers "a source of regional pride."[10] A speaker from the Brookings Institution at the 1962 AUU meeting declared that "the task of the university is to establish the educated use of urbanization, in order to transform civic energy into creative cultural change and economic development."[11] William Carlson, president of Toledo University, published a book, also in 1962, on municipal universities, asserting that the programs of municipal and urban universities must "meet the needs of their respective communities as manufacturing and commercial centers" and as centers of arts and culture.[12]

The leaders of colleges in cities led an expanding national debate on the implications of the democratization of higher education. Although some students in small towns and rural areas commuted to college, the discussion about commuters and part-time students focused on cities. Increasingly, leaders in higher education came to define the "urban university" as an institution serving working-class and minority students who lived at home. In a society now predominantly metropolitan, they no longer talked explicitly about the negative influences of the city itself, and only occasionally about the importance of a countrified campus. Now they focused more sharply on the problems inherent in trying to educate nonresident students.

In their meetings and publications, higher education leaders in the postwar era often echoed their prewar predecessors' view that working-class commuters and students from immigrant families needed special attention because of their urban upbringing, their lack of refinement, and their inability to experience the life of a campus community. Addressing the annual meeting of the AUU in 1946, Ordway Tead, chairman of the New York City Board of Education, urged his audience to educate students for "urbanity . . . for rounded, effective, capable, gracious capacity to live and work with others for the city's good." He said that he received a report written by Brooklyn College faculty and staff members that said, "Too many intellectually advanced but social restricted individuals have graduated from Brooklyn College *summa cum laude* only to rate *magna cum difficultate* in daily life."[13] In the same year, the newly appointed president of Wells College for women in Aurora, New York, Richard Leighton Greene, told trustees and alumnae at a Waldorf-Astoria dinner that someone had recently "branded the whole idea of 'going away to college' as a relic of an aristocracy which we have left behind us." He responded by saying this was "like some people's objections to good manners."[14]

Alfred Nelson, interim chancellor of the University of Denver, told the AUU three years later that urban university students lacked a sense of "close campus unity" and that their lives were "community centered rather than college centered."[15] Two years after that, the president of the American Council on Education, Arthur Adams, urged AUU members to give greater attention to "the cultivation of [a] sense of belongingness," which "can be acquired so easily by living on a rural campus."[16] And the next year, Victor Spathelf, president of Ferris Institute (now Ferris State University) in Big Rapids, Michigan, told his colleagues that the "uniquely heterogeneous population at urban universities" required programs of cultural enrichment, religious and spiritual development, comprehensive health services, and special efforts to involve students in campus activities.[17] In a 1955 history of Brooklyn College, the college's former dean quoted approvingly a senior professor's characterization of the institution's students. "The greatest weakness of the Brooklyn College students . . . is their incompetence in easy, courteous, persuasive human relations."[18] In his address at the 1959 AUU meeting, Chancellor Furniss, having extolled the virtues of an urban location, went on to say that for an urban institution to "have the strength of character of a true university," it must have "at least an appreciable portion of the student body from out of town [and] resident in the university community."[19]

Meanwhile, the Ford Foundation began planning a program to address the growing problems of American cities through higher education. An internal memo stated that for the foundation's purposes, an "urban university" meant "a university situated within a city and drawing its student body predominantly from the city and the associated metropolitan area" and that therefore a substantial portion of the student body would commute to campus. The nation needed "a substantial improvement in both the actual quality and the prestige of the typical urban university." One Ford staff member reported unhappily that the University of Pennsylvania had decided to promote itself as a residential university "in the Ivy League pattern" and to "leave the education of the local youth to other institutions," creating tensions with the Philadelphia public high school system.[20]

A good number of faculty articulated similar concerns about the inadequacy of urban commuter students. In 1963, David Boroff, a young English professor

Houston Hall, University of Pennsylvania, c. 1904. Courtesy of the Library of Congress Prints & Photographs Online Catalog (digital ID LC-D4-17531).

at New York University, published an article in the *New York Times* lauding the learning opportunities for college students in New York City. But he went on to assert that commuter students in the city's municipal universities "are in New York City but not really of it." These students "tend to identify less with the city as a whole than with their particular neighborhoods in Brooklyn, the Bronx or Queens. . . . Not having left home, they tend to stay home spiritually." In the same year, sociologist Martin Trow asserted that democratization of higher education in America had lowered academic standards in some institutions and "brings into higher education more of the listlessness and boredom of students who are not highly motivated but who are just 'doing time.'" However, he did not direct this criticism specifically to colleges in cities.[21] As late as 1963, an education professor who also served as graduate dean of Florida State University published an analysis of "urban sprawl" in academia, arguing that the development of intellectual potential in most college students "depends on changes in values and motivations," which are modified through personal contacts with professors. Construction of more campus housing would help, but he also urged that the institutions could, in numerous ways, establish "informal student groups that will promote the goals of the institution."[22]

Mental health professionals and student counselors shared these views as well as other concerns about commuters. The *Journal of Higher Education* published an article in 1945 arguing that the responsibilities of student advisers at the rapidly expanded city colleges presented "new circumstances" and therefore "new problems." A low-income graduate, the authors argued, faced a "sorry dilemma": how "to explain to his hopeful mother or father that his education prepares him for a successful life in which earning and livelihood is only a part?"[23] Respondents to a 1955 survey of college counselors reported that commuters had weak campus ties, delayed maturation, and "less opportunity to develop social skills and confidence."[24]

By the early 1960s, few still believed that a college education required a discrete campus in the country or a small town, but many still insisted that students must engage in the campus community to build character and social skill. Indeed, the growth of nonresident student enrollment in cities reinforced the longstanding concern that commuter students, even if academically capable, lacked refinement and interpersonal sophistication.

This reinforced the idea that the term "urban university" meant an institution serving working-class commuter students. Indeed, in 1963, a researcher reported to AUU attendees the results of interviews of some twenty AUU member presidents. In four or five cases, the president or executive vice president "disclaimed any part of this 'urban university association.'" He also reported, "A number of university presidents were reluctant to admit that theirs were truly urban institutions. Many claimed to be something better or more than that." And "only three or four . . . said, 'Yes, this is an urban institution. We are proud of it.'"[25]

Urban Studies Initiatives

Nonetheless, in the postwar years the leaders of universities in cities argued ever-more emphatically that their institutions needed to use their scholarly expertise to address the growing challenges facing their cities. In the years before World War II, universities focused such efforts primarily on training city government workers and gathering data on specific issues faced by the municipalities. Now this research broadened considerably.

Columbia University, for example, created an Institute for Urban Land Use and Housing Studies, drawing on faculty from business, law, architecture, and the social sciences. The institute identified several initial research projects reflecting issues confronting New York and many other cities. These included the problems of urban redevelopment, public housing, financing private housing, management of large-scale housing projects, and collecting better statistics on land use and housing.[26] The University of Pennsylvania began planning a similar entity, the Institute of Urban Studies, during World War II. Initiated by the Department of Land and City Planning of the School of Fine Arts, it brought together faculty from a range of departments across the university. The dean of fine arts recruited a faculty member from Columbia involved with its land use and housing institute as co-director.[27] Soon after its founding, the institute received support from the Ford Foundation and other funders to study the history of city planning and landscape design, resulting in the publication of a five-volume history authored by the distinguished architectural scholar Edwin A. Gutkind.[28] In 1958, MIT launched a PhD program in city planning. Meanwhile, the Rockefeller Foundation decided that it should not limit foundation support for the study of city planning to the social sciences. Determined to find "how ideas and actions might better serve urban life, including cultural and human values," they gave funds to Jane Jacobs, a popular writer on urban issues who at this time held a faculty position at the New School for Social Research, to study "how architectural forms and lay-out can better provide for human functions."[29]

City College of New York undertook a much broader initiative at this time. The College-Community program, started in 1948, focused initially on the campus neighborhood in north Harlem, whose residents were mostly black. The college president declared that the community surrounding the campus "offers a definite challenge to the college to bring its resources to bear upon the problems presented" and also presents the opportunity to create "a large and varied laboratory" for the departments of sociology, education, hygiene, psychology, and student life.

City College also initiated an interdisciplinary MA program with a specialization on the New York metropolitan area. A brochure for students explained that in addition to studying urbanization in America, the program focused on "that most remarkable of all municipal phenomena, the emergence of the City of New York and its environs." The Rockefeller Foundation supplied funds to develop courses on New York, and the Littauer Foundation supported development of the MA program. The program also undertook a range of research projects to study "the New York Area as a viable community." Studies included the history of the emergence of "Greater New York" at the end of the nineteenth century; reform movements; centralization and decentralization in New York government; manufacturing and retail; the impact of art, literature, and music; and class stratification in the metropolitan area.[30] UCLA's Bureau of Governmental Research shared CCNY's metropolitan-focused research, requesting funding, unsuccessfully, from the Carnegie Corporation to study the factors blocking development of a metropolitan government plan for greater Los Angeles.[31]

Given the growing interest in urban research at universities in cities, in 1958 the Social Science Research Council established a committee on urbanization.

Dedication of City College of New York, 1908. The campus opened in 1906. Courtesy of the Library of Congress Prints & Photographs Online Catalog (digital ID LC-B2-77-4).

In 1965, the committee joined with the University of Chicago to sponsor a conference on studying urbanization. The *American Behavioral Scientist* devoted an entire issue to "Urban Studies Reconsidered." One article summarized important new works in the field, and another described the work of urban studies centers across the country. An article on urban research argued that scholars writing on this subject did not have clear goals because of "the lack of common goals in metropolitan regions." A writer on urban studies graduate education emphasized the need for a close relationship between urbanists and professionals who served city residents. Others discussed the status of urban extension, the development of scientific approaches to urban planning, and urban studies internationally. The issue editors argued that the term "urban" had become "a powerful force in uniting heretofore unrelated academic approaches" and that despite criticism from some scholars that it was driven by outside funders, "urban studies represents a truly important new dimension of higher education."[32]

A few urban policy leaders dissented from this view. Jack Vaughn, president of the National Urban Coalition, told a meeting of university public relations officers in 1971 that "the university should be very careful about getting into the field of problem solving" because it should be committed to "living and thinking for the long term, not for immediate utility." He expressed deep concern about racism and the problems of cities, but he insisted that universities should serve the cities by "unmasking everything that is a sham" but "not by trying to solve society's social problems."[33] Few other urban policy advocates shared this view, however.

Urban Renewal and Neighborhood Relations

Even as urban university scholars advanced the study of cities and metropolitan areas, the massive outflow of city residents of moderate income to low-density suburbs and the inflow of southern black, Puerto Rican, and Mexican migrants to commercial and industrial cities posed a real challenge to urban colleges. Convinced that the safety and attractiveness of their neighborhoods played a critical role in addressing the problems of deteriorating cities, they participated actively in urban renewal projects, seeing these as a natural extension of their commitment to community service. In 1957, the Association of American Universities (AAU) announced that it planned to initiate an extensive nationwide study "to determine what can be done to halt the deterioration of neighborhoods adjacent to urban universities" and how these universities could preserve "the traditional college environment of city-bound campuses." The Association of Urban Universities readily agreed to cosponsor this study.

At the AUU's annual meeting in 1958, Paul Ylvisaker, associate director of the Public Affairs program at the Ford Foundation, described the "plight of the urban university," which has been "left behind to inherit a neighborhood growing steadily less desirable." Under these circumstances, these institutions "will be sorely tempted to join the flight from the city," but he insisted that to do so would "deny the purpose and potential of the urban university." Then Julian Levi, executive director of the South East Chicago Commission, created by the University of Chicago to address the decline of the neighborhood adjacent to the campus, argued that campus neighborhoods should attract middle-class residents not only to benefit the university but to counteract the city's decline. Cities, he argued, need universities whose faculty live in and engage with their communities. They also need the scientific, educational, and cultural institutions that locate themselves adjacent to universities.[34]

The committee overseeing the AAU study included the presidents of Columbia, Harvard, and the University of Pennsylvania. It sought to address three problems: the lack of room for expansion, the threat posed by slums and crime to students and faculty, and the high costs of addressing these.[35] Still another higher education organization, the American Council on Education, appointed a Special Committee on Urban Renewal in 1959, and the next year set up an office to assist individual universities in urban renewal projects.[36]

From the inception of federally financed urban renewal in 1949, some universities negotiated neighborhood redevelopment projects with their city governments and sought federal funds for this purpose. As a result of vigorous lobbying by the University of Chicago and others, the US Housing Act of 1959 greatly expanded these opportunities. Section 112 of the act provided that for every dollar an educational institution spent for land acquisition, demolition, building rehabilitation, or relocation of occupants of demolished buildings adjacent to or in the vicinity of an urban renewal project, the city could receive two to three dollars of federal urban renewal money. This created a powerful incentive for universities to work with city government on campus neighborhood projects and to negotiate an allocation of city funds for the university projects. After the 1959 amendment, the American Council on Education's Special Committee on Urban Renewal worked to draft a model state law that would remove obstacles to maximum federal support in several states.[37] By 1964, the federal Housing and Home Finance Agency reported that 154 urban renewal projects involving 120 colleges and universities and 75 hospitals had received section 112 funds.[38]

The Illinois Institute of Technology pioneered in addressing the deterioration of its surrounding neighborhood. After considering a move to the suburbs, it decided in the mid-1930s to build its campus at the site of the former Armour Institute, on the city's south side, a neighborhood populated largely by poor blacks. Along with nearby Michael Reese Hospital, it helped establish the private nonprofit South Side Redevelopment Agency in 1945, renamed the Planning Board in 1946. This organization, led largely by IIT, viewed black residents as the primary victims of neighborhood blight, which caused their housing to deteriorate and produced poverty, prostitution, and juvenile delinquency. As the group developed various residential and commercial projects for the area, IIT grew its campus from seven to sixty-five acres, razing numerous structures.[39]

From its opening in 1892, the University of Chicago, located to the south of IIT, stood in a residential neighborhood that was also home to most of its faculty. University officials viewed faculty residence as a great asset. In 1945, Chancellor Robert Hutchins reported in his state of the university address that the Hyde Park neighborhood had been deteriorating for fifteen years and therefore the university had "the worst-housed faculty in the United States." Undergraduate student enrollment had declined from 3,200 to 1,300 by the early 1950s. Hutchins's successor, Lawrence Kimpton, established the South East Chicago Commission (SECC) in 1952 to "combat the forces of uncertainty and deterioration at work in the neighborhood." This meant fighting crime, organizing civic involvement among the citizens of each block, and developing an overall plan for the neighborhood and its improvement. At base, it sought to maintain and expand the area's middle-class population and racial integration. In practical terms, this meant restricting the growing population of low-income African Americans in housing surrounding the campus.

In 1956, Kimpton got the city government to begin work with the university to develop the Hyde Park-Kenwood urban renewal plan. Two years later, the plan won unanimous approval from the Chicago City Council. The plan rezoned 80 percent of Hyde Park land for residence instead of commerce. Kimpton's successor, George Beadle, continued this program of neighborhood renewal, demolishing deteriorated buildings, acquiring property for university expansion, and fostering new middle-class housing construction. By the early 1960s, the University of Chicago had purchased 10 percent of the neighborhood's rental units. The university also persuaded the Illinois Synod of the Lutheran Church to merge several of its schools into the Lutheran School of Theology in Hyde Park.

The university's renewal program faced growing opposition from black neighborhood residents, some of whom organized in opposition to the Lutheran seminary. In 1962, the Congress of Racial Equality organized a sit-in at the university's administration building to protest efforts to reduce the neighborhood's black population. One analyst, writing for an architectural journal in 1963, reported that the University of Chicago and SECC "stirred up a hornet's nest of opposition" in largely black southwest Hyde Park, which the university had targeted for its expansion, and in the Woodlawn neighborhood, just south of Hyde Park, whose residents formed the Woodlawn Organization (TWO) to fight university expansion south of the Midway.[40]

In 1947, Columbia University joined with David Rockefeller (whose family owned substantial property in Morningside Heights), Union Theological Seminary, the Jewish Theological Seminary, the Church of St. John the Divine, St. Luke's Hospital, the Julliard School, and two Catholic churches to found Morningside Heights Inc. The neighborhood's residents were not nearly as poor as those who lived in the area around IIT, but some parts of the neighborhood had clearly deteriorated, and street crime was extremely high. In the early 1950s, Morningside Heights Inc., led largely by Columbia, worked with the local police precinct to reduce crime and to combat juvenile gangs. It focused primarily, however, on getting investors to buy and renovate or demolish deteriorating buildings. The organization brought about construction of Morningside Gardens, a new housing cooperative with tenants as shareholders, and supported the construction of new public housing. It also gave mortgage support to investors to buy up deteriorated buildings. Columbia and some of the other institutions ended up buying a great number of these buildings, which they later used for institutional expansion.[41]

Columbia also built an athletic field at the southeast end of Morningside Park in the 1950s and initiated improvements in other parts of the park to be used by both Columbia students and community residents. The university spent about $200,000 on these projects. The city Parks Department agreed to maintain these facilities, which included two baseball fields, three touch football fields, and a soccer field.

Despite these efforts, some Columbia administrators and faculty remained deeply worried about the fate of the neighborhood. In 1930 few blacks or Puerto

Ricans had lived in Morningside Heights, although Columbia administrators had already expressed concern about its closeness to Harlem. By the 1950s, 6,652 Puerto Ricans and 6,671 African Americans lived there. Dean Jacques Barzun described the late 1950s and early 1960s as "the era of the packed suitcase" for Columbia professors, suggesting that the decline of the campus neighborhood caused top faculty to leave. According to a faculty member in the psychology department, a senior colleague left in 1956 because "the blacks got too much for him." Columbia's director of campus planning, Stanley Salmen, referred to the new residents moving into Morningside Heights as a "dirty group" and "an unsettled population, always pressing to secure cheap accommodations."[42]

The University of Pennsylvania perceived similar problems in its neighborhood. In the late 1940s, its trustees considered moving to Valley Forge, where the university owned a substantial amount of land, but they decided against it. University leaders in 1955 began discussing the "deteriorating neighborhood" surrounding the university, which had a growing black population. President Gaylord Harnwell expressed anxiety that faculty and students increasingly declined to live in the campus neighborhood. In 1956, a Penn professor of urban planning, Martin Meyerson, proposed that the university undertake a vigorous program of West Philadelphia redevelopment and revitalization to keep the neighborhood "from becoming a sea of residential slums and commercial and institutional islands."[43] In 1970, Meyerson was appointed university president.

Two years later, the university and several neighboring institutions, including Drexel, began planning a corporation that could address these problems and take advantage of federal urban renewal money. In 1959, they created the West Philadelphia Corporation for the newly renamed University City neighborhood. Its activities included advocating for code enforcement; improved city services and schools; stimulating investment in the neighborhood for new and renovated housing; attracting professional, business, and research organizations to the area; improving local public schools; and encouraging residents to put down roots and show pride in their community. The efforts of Columbia and the University of Chicago to change their neighborhoods deeply influenced President Harnwell. Like them, Penn wanted to ensure that large numbers of students and faculty lived close to campus.[44]

In the early 1950s, administrators at Temple University, located about two miles north of downtown Philadelphia, were also troubled about their neighborhood. The population of poor African Americans and Puerto Ricans was growing rapidly. Commuter students from the Philadelphia metropolitan area

Broad Street in Philadelphia, 1922, before it was razed for construction by Temple University.

constituted a large majority of the student body, but few low income and minority students from North Philadelphia enrolled at Temple. The university acquired a large parcel of land in suburban Chestnut Hill and seriously considered moving there. In 1955 the university decided to stay in Philadelphia, partly as a result of an agreement with the city to use urban renewal to acquire land needed for expansion. Temple's president, Millard Gladfelter, envisioned transforming what he called "an ugly, blighted area" into "an attractive, park-like oasis, upon which will rise many handsome, modern buildings surrounded by beautiful shade trees, and spacious green lawns," thereby contributing to the city's aesthetic and cultural assets.[45]

Four years after Columbia created Morningside Heights Inc., nine institutions in Cleveland began efforts to advance systematic planning and collaboration for the area known as University Circle. The neighborhood, where Western Reserve had chosen to locate at the time of its founding, was also home to Case Institute of Technology, which later would merge with Western

Conwell Hall (*right*) and Carnell Hall (*left*), Temple University, 1937; on Broad Street site razed in 1922. Special Collections Research Center, Temple University Libraries, Philadelphia, PA.

Reserve, as well as the Cleveland Museum of Art, the Cleveland Symphony Orchestra, the Cleveland Institute of Art, the Cleveland Institute of Music, the Western Reserve Historical Society, the Cleveland Museum of Natural History, University Hospital, and several medical institutions. In 1956, they put together the University Circle Development Foundation (UCDF) to coordinate activities and plan for future development.

UCDF leaders determined that residential areas bordering on two sides of the circle and a commercial area on another side showed "signs of incipient decay," but they argued that a coherent plan for further development of University Circle "would be a powerful stabilizing influence" for these immediately adjacent neighborhoods. The universities had a huge stake in this planning process because they would need to acquire land and build new facilities to a much greater extent than most of the other entities. In light of the decline of traditional manufacturing in Cleveland, UCDF argued that the presence of the universities made University Circle an excellent location for attracting businesses that depended on brain power. UCDF did encounter significant opposition from local residents for some of its proposed projects. A longstanding Italian-American neighborhood known as Little Italy undertook aggressive protests and lobbying when UCDF proposed a state law that would enable it to exercise eminent domain over property owners who refused to sell. Several blocks away, in a middle-class black area bordering Western Reserve, the neighborhood association joined with the residents of Little Italy in opposing the extension of eminent domain. UCDF withdrew its proposed legislation when it became clear that it would not succeed.[46]

Fordham University in the Bronx experienced considerable strain as large numbers of low-income black and Puerto Rican residents moved to its neighborhood. Fordham also owned an old building on Broadway in Manhattan that housed its law school and a few other programs. Fordham's president, who had ties to Robert Moses, the city's master planner, decided to purchase 320,000 square feet in a low-income neighborhood adjoining the southwest corner of Central Park, in what is now Lincoln Center. Moses planned to rebuild the area as the new home of the Metropolitan Opera, the New York Philharmonic, and other performance groups. Fordham received two-thirds of the purchase cost through the 1959 amendment to the Housing Act. Tenants, homeowners, and small-business owners who would be displaced protested and challenged Fordham's Lincoln Center plans in court, albeit unsuccessfully. The new law school building, the first of several Fordham buildings in the area, opened in 1961.[47]

In 1962, Duquesne University in Pittsburgh received federal urban renewal funds to acquire twenty acres of cleared land for major expansion of the campus, rental housing, green open space, and parking. Pittsburgh mayor Joseph Barr supported this project enthusiastically, noting that the enlarged university would employ 325 additional people. In the same year, Georgia State University began a similar renewal project, working closely with the city of Atlanta. Numerous other universities had the same need to acquire land for expansion and to improve their neighborhoods.[48]

In 1962, William L. Slayton, commissioner of the US Urban Renewal Administration, declared university-city collaboration critical to the revitalization of central cities. He stated that universities were growing faster than other sectors of the economy, that jobs and student spending greatly helped municipalities, and that universities played a critical role in attracting research and technologically based industry to cities.[49]

Urban renewal involving higher education institutions became a major tool in efforts to address the problems of central cities. Universities would continue these activities in the coming decades. Although university leaders and city officials viewed neighborhood improvement projects as critical in addressing the decline of central cities, they greatly increased tensions with local residents.

Tensions among Universities

The great expansion of demand for a college education in the postwar years caused many states to launch new urban institutions or to transform teachers colleges or extension programs in cities into full-scale colleges and universities. This aspect of the democratization of higher education brought about considerable conflict with land-grant and other established state research universities, reflecting once again the anti-urban orientation of American higher education.

This conflict emerged first in California. In 1919, the California legislature passed a bill creating in Los Angeles a "southern branch" of the University of California. It transferred the California State Normal School of Los Angeles, started in 1881, to the University of California. The normal school, which offered a two-year teacher preparation program in downtown LA, now became the state university's new southern branch. University president Benjamin Ide

Wheeler, alumni, and northern California legislators had opposed this legislation. But community leaders in Los Angeles supported it strongly, and donors committed funds to purchase a large tract of farmland in Westwood, an area near Hollywood, to build a new campus. In 1927, the University of California regents renamed the campus the University of California at Los Angeles. The campus head had the title of "provost" and reported to the university president in Berkeley. A 1948 report on the university's governance explained that authority over campus budgets, personnel, and most other matters rested with the president and concluded that this extreme centralization produced enormous inefficiencies. However, President Robert Sproul remained committed to the concept of "One University" and feared that giving more authority to the Los Angeles provost would threaten institutional unity. In 1951, the provost title at UCLA and Berkeley changed to chancellor. In theory this created the multicampus statewide university system, although much authority remained centralized in the president's office.[50]

After World War II, the University of Illinois in Champaign-Urbana set up an extension program at Navy Pier in Chicago, providing the first two years of college to veterans. By the 1950s, it had become clear that the university needed a campus in the Chicago area, but leaders of the university in Champaign-Urbana worried that a Chicago campus could compete with the flagship for funding. Moreover, several of the private universities in the city, including DePaul, Loyola, Roosevelt, and the Illinois Institute of Technology feared that a Chicago campus of the state's flagship public university would draw students from them.

David Henry, a former president of Wayne University and an active member of the AUU, became president of the University of Illinois in 1955. He strongly supported development of a Chicago-area campus committed to educational opportunity for local students and service to the community, which he believed was the proper mission of an urban university. Initially, he sought to locate the campus in a western suburb, believing that many suburban students would not travel to the "dangerous" central city. He had considered relocating Wayne University to a suburb after the 1943 Detroit race riots. This experience undoubtedly influenced his views about the location of the Chicago area campus. Mayor Richard Daley, a longtime advocate of a public university in Chicago, insisted that the campus be built near downtown, and he prevailed. Despite the belief of Henry and others that the Chicago area "urban university" should focus on undergraduate education, it emerged as a comprehensive research university with a strong commitment to the city.[51]

The University of Wisconsin in Madison offered a modest number of freshman and sophomore courses at an extension program in Milwaukee. Milwaukee State College, part of a state college system, had long offered instruction to teachers in the city. The University of Wisconsin vigorously opposed the establishment of a full university in Milwaukee. The possibility of merging the extension program and the teachers college, and the separate but related issue of creating a public research university in the state's largest city, had been under discussion since the late 1940s. In 1955, the Wisconsin legislature merged the Wisconsin State College of Milwaukee with the Milwaukee extension program of the University of Wisconsin. It also appointed a Coordinating Committee for Higher Education to oversee all state colleges and universities. The University of Wisconsin had opposed a statewide system, arguing that it would diminish the university's high standards. And it continued to insist that its two-year program in Milwaukee should not be expanded, that students who wanted to study beyond that level should do so in Madison. According to J. Martin Klotsche, only when the University of Wisconsin recognized that some expansion was inevitable "did it grudgingly concede to develop a four year program" but "with the clear understanding that professional work would be narrowly limited and graduate study would be carried out under the close supervision of the Madison campus."[52]

The 1955 law specified that the new university in Milwaukee would be headed by a provost reporting to the president. Klotsche, who had served as president of the state college in Milwaukee since 1946, became provost of the University of Wisconsin–Milwaukee when it opened. His title changed to chancellor in 1965. In 1963, Klotsche and university president Fred Harvey Harrington, at the request of the board of regents, submitted a set of proposals for the future of UWM. The proposals stated that it should within twenty years achieve "major university status."[53]

In Massachusetts, the large number of private colleges and universities, many in Boston, lobbied for years against the development and expansion of the state university, which began instruction in Amherst it 1863 as the land-grant Massachusetts Agricultural College. Renamed Massachusetts State College in 1931, the state did not broaden it to a full university until 1947, when it changed its name again, this time to the University of Massachusetts.

As enrollment pressure grew through the 1950s, many people argued that Massachusetts needed a public university in Boston. A public teachers college, begun as a city normal school in 1862, became a state institution in 1952. However, Boston had no public comprehensive university. A committee of faculty and administrators at the University of Massachusetts prepared a long-range plan in 1962 that opposed establishment of a Boston "branch campus." But in 1964, the University of Massachusetts president told members of the legislature that the university would need to reject eight thousand of the twelve thousand applicants for freshman admission. This created significant political pressure, and the president of the Massachusetts senate introduced legislation providing an appropriation for a new Boston branch. The university's president told the trustees that UMass-Boston would be "a quality institution which eventually, like UCLA, may grow to 20,000 or 25,000 students." The presidents of Northeastern and Boston University unsuccessfully opposed the plan. The Boston campus opened in 1965, headed by a chancellor.[54]

In 1946, the state of New Jersey merged the privately funded University of Newark with Rutgers University in New Brunswick, at that time a quasi-public land-grant institution. Under this new structure, the Newark colleges reported to a Newark campus vice president, a title later changed to provost, who reported to the university president in New Brunswick. In a history of Rutgers-Newark, historian Harold Wechsler explained that "this was not a merger of equals" and that control quickly shifted from "the banks of the Passaic" in Newark to the banks of the Raritan in New Brunswick.[55] In short, as the democratization of American higher education advanced in the postwar years, necessitating more and more colleges in cities, some leaders of universities drew on higher education's anti-urban tradition to try to protect their institutions from competition.

In the first decades of the twentieth century, higher education institutions in cities had pioneered in democratizing college access and in developing, with some ambivalence, the idea that college education did not require campus residence. In the years after World War II, as college attendance expanded vastly, nonresidential education, begun largely by colleges in cities, became the American norm. As the problems of central cities received increasing national concern, universities greatly expanded research on cities, and academic programs in urban studies grew substantially. University faculty and students also increased their service to local agencies and residents. Federal programs

Former brewery at 40 Rector Street, c. 1950, which housed the University of Newark before and for several years after it became part of Rutgers University.

designed to address the deterioration of the central city enabled private institutions to begin the process, albeit controversial, of upgrading their neighborhoods. This growing engagement of universities in their urban communities further strengthened American higher education's commitment to service as a core mission.

Yet despite the growing dominance of urban institutions in shaping American higher education, its anti-urban tradition continued, albeit in more subtle ways. Debates about the definition and role of an urban university continued, with the term "urban university" increasingly understood to mean a working-class commuter institution. The longstanding concerns about the city's negative influence on students diminished, but issues regarding commuters and ethnic minorities still received much attention. Anti-urbanism also played a key role in the efforts of flagship state universities to prevent the creation of new public research institutions in major cities. The coming of the "urban crisis" in the 1960s and 1970s would greatly accelerate these trends.

4

Response to the Urban Crisis, 1964–1980

By the mid-1960s, government leaders, journalists, scholars, policy analysts, and civil rights and social justice activists routinely used the term "urban crisis" to describe the growing problems of American cities. The decline of central cities could be seen partly in population statistics. Between 1950 and 1970, cities grew by 10 million people, but the population of the suburbs increased by 85 million. By 1970, 37.6 percent of all Americans lived in suburbs, twice the percentage in 1940, while 31 percent lived in cities. Industrial cities suffered the greatest losses as manufacturers relocated to areas with lower density and cheaper land.

In the 1970s, Cincinnati lost 15 percent of its population; Detroit, 21 percent; and St. Louis, 27 percent. When three steel mills in Youngstown, Ohio, shut down, it eliminated twenty thousand jobs. Akron lost its automobile tire factories and nearly forty thousand jobs. In 1972, steel plants in Gary, Indiana, substantially reduced production, resulting in a 40 percent unemployment rate. Larger cities also experienced substantial job losses. Between 1969 and 1976, New York City saw 542,000 factory, office, and retail jobs depart.[1]

This loss of jobs, the decline of population growth, and the movement of more and more middle-class people to the suburbs greatly reduced municipal tax revenues, creating severe financial crises for many city governments. New York City's debt crisis received the greatest attention. By 1974, New York had accumulated a $3 billion budget deficit, forcing it to borrow money to pay employee salaries and provide basic services. Financial support from the federal government and the state ultimately prevented bankruptcy.

The continuing loss of jobs and middle-class residents coupled with the negative effects of urban renewal and public housing contributed to rapidly rising urban crime. Although violent crime increased across the country, cities accounted for the largest share by far. The national homicide rate doubled between 1962 and 1972. Robberies and illegal drug use also increased dramatically, especially in low-income ghetto neighborhoods. By the late 1960s, for example, 13 percent of Washington, DC, males born in 1953 had become heroin addicts; in the city's poorest areas, that number increased to 25 percent.[2]

In many cities, low-income residents, mostly black, engaged in major civil disturbances, commonly referred to at the time as "race riots," provoked largely by tension between black males and white police officers. In 1964, after a police officer in Harlem shot and killed a fifteen-year-old African-American, blacks attacked whites and set fire to many buildings. Shortly thereafter, similar disturbances broke out in Brooklyn's Bedford-Stuyvesant neighborhood. The following year, a major disturbance in the Watts area of Los Angeles killed thirty-four people and injured over a thousand, with six hundred buildings damaged by arson. In the next few years, similar events occurred in Chicago, Philadelphia, Detroit, Newark, and many other cities.[3]

Civil rights advocates sought programs to address the urban crisis as a natural extension of their efforts to fight segregation and discrimination. President Lyndon Johnson undertook several major initiatives to address the problems of poor people in cities and discrimination against African Americans. On May 22, 1964, he declared that "Our society will never be great until our cities are great."

Many people, both within and outside of higher education, argued that universities in cities had a significant role to play in response to the urban crisis. The Association of Urban Universities devoted much of its conference time to the crisis facing cities. For example, Edward Litchfield, chancellor of the University of Pittsburgh, told attendees at the 1964 annual meeting that universities should not "regard themselves merely as educational institutions" but as "vehicles for doing things [in cities] that wouldn't otherwise be done."[4]

The crisis of the cities sparked numerous academic conferences on the university's role in mitigating city problems. In 1965, the American Council on Education sponsored a meeting of educators, public officials, and civic leaders at Wayne State University. The *Educational Record* published the speeches given at the conference in a special issue. Paul Yvisker of the Ford Foundation argued that universities must serve as "an early warning system" for society. He argued that proper research could forecast urban ills: "We could have anticipated the turmoil that now accompanies the Negro's struggle for equality. We could have predicted the problems we now face in educating deprived children in the central city. We could even have anticipated the great migration of the suburbs since the 1940s and the concomitant problems of urban blight." Other conference participants included Massachusetts Institute of Technology political scientist Robert Wood, speaking on "the new metropolis and the new university" and Detroit mayor Jerome Cavanagh on the growth of the American city.[5]

Boston University hosted a 1967 conference, "The University in Urban Society." One of its five speakers, a professor who had previously directed a bureau of the Office of Economic Opportunity, argued that the urgency of the country's escalating urban problems "requires the increased assumption of responsibility by universities for rapidly increasing our knowledge of urban life and urban problems."[6]

The state of Illinois received a federal grant to conduct seven conferences "to train consultants to citizen groups." Northern Illinois University published the papers from its 1967 conference, including the opening address, "College-Community Participation in Solving Urban Problems."[7] The University of California Medical Center hosted a conference in the same year at which a University of San Francisco professor called for universities in every major city to establish citywide consortia that would "provide the major thrust of the individual institution's commitment to social justice in the urban environment."[8] Also in 1967, other units of the University of California, San Francisco held a similar conference on the role of higher education in city vitality. A speaker outlining "a new approach" to higher education, explained that "the university, and only the university, can be so innovative, can take an over-all view of the urban scene . . . with a total concern for the city."[9]

In 1969, the *Bulletin of the American Academy of Arts and Sciences* summarized an address at its annual meeting by SUNY Buffalo president Martin Meyerson, who had previously headed the MIT-Harvard Joint Center for Urban Studies. Meyerson urged the "creation of a climate within the university that would advance knowledge of urban life [and] develop alternative policy questions."[10]

The American Council on Education (ACE) hosted a meeting in 1970 entitled "The Campus and the Racial Crisis." In 1974, with support from the US Department of Housing and Urban Development, it sponsored programs in Washington, San Francisco, Chicago, and New Orleans on urban involvement in higher education. One of the speakers in New Orleans, the president of Texas Southern University, argued that "urban involvement must not be regarded as an 'attractive alternative' for higher education, but as being organic to the traditional functions of the university."[11] ACE published an interpretive summary of the four conferences, stating that "college and university administrators are virtually unanimous in the view that urban involvement should be a function of higher education," but it also indicated that higher education had not reached any agreement on how to define its urban involvement.[12]

Higher educators in various books and articles made the same call for university attention to the crisis of cities. Eric Cox, writing in the *Educational Record* in 1964 about "the social decay confronting our cities," reported that "the size and quality of city problems in the 1960s are of such scope and breadth that communities are looking to universities for aid."[13] Paul Reinert, president of Saint Louis University, in a book entitled *The Urban Catholic University*, wrote that cities have faced "fantastically complicated problems," and therefore urban universities "must become intellectual citadels . . . of the urban age."[14] In 1970, an education research organization published a summary of academic writing and a bibliography on universities and cities. The author explained that "while urban universities have grown and prospered, the cities surrounding them have deteriorated." In reviewing the writings on this subject, he found that "most of the literature favors involvement" and that "a great deal of it expresses the theme that the university 'can, must, and should' do something for the welfare of the city."[15] In a 1976 publication, University of Alabama at Birmingham president Joseph F. Volker held that "the responsibility of a comprehensive, urban university is responding to the needs and maintaining the confidence of the community which it serves."[16]

Higher education organizations also devoted considerable time and resources to encouraging and assisting their member institutions to address the urban crisis. In 1970 the ACE established an Office of Urban Affairs to promote involvement in cities and to aid members in getting involved. The office hosted meetings for senior administrators and distributed guides to institutional self-study of engagement with urban affairs and to federal funding of university engagement with cities. It also surveyed the urban affairs activities of other college and university organizations. Fifty-five of eighty higher education associations responded to the 1971 ACE survey. Of those responding, 87 percent had, or anticipated having, some urban-related activities. However, the ACE's report described most of these activities as superficial and unlikely to have much impact, with only nineteen association programs demonstrating real concern with cities.

In 1973, the ACE conducted a direct survey of colleges and universities, sending questionnaires to 519 institutions, a 20 percent sample of institutions in cities or adjacent suburbs. Seventy-two percent of respondents agreed that urban involvement should constitute a major function of American higher education, but only 31 percent said that their own institution defined it as a central institutional activity. And 34 percent said they had difficulty determining what kinds of urban activities seemed appropriate.[17]

The *New York Times* ran several articles in this period echoing the call for universities to address the urban crisis. A 1964 editorial praised a large Ford Foundation grant to New York University because it "puts the spotlight on the need to speed the private universities' involvement in the life and death struggle of the nation's cities."[18] In 1966, it reported that University of Pennsylvania president Gaylord Harnwell called on the nation's urban universities "to mobilize their resources 'for solutions to the revolutions that are shaking urban society'" because these constituted "the last major institutions of urban life that can be called upon for unbiased, dispassionate information concerning the urban crisis and its solution."[19] Two years later, Columbia University urban planning professor Charles Abrams insisted that urban universities had to engage actively in their communities: "It's either service or the university has to retreat somewhere into a forest."[20]

Critics and Defenders of University Responses to the Urban Crisis

In the years of the urban crisis, most higher education leaders agreed that universities should address the problems of cities in appropriate ways, even as they sought to moderate public expectations of what universities realistically could do. A few academicians in the late 1960s explicitly criticized universities for their failure to respond to the needs of cities. A publication of the University of Missouri's Extension Division accused universities of neglecting "the present and anticipated future of urban problems."[21] The authors of a publication from Boston University's Metrocenter observed that universities "have fled the cities for the countryside" and those that remained in the city have built ivory towers "to shut out the city and its life." These towers "have not been built only of stone; they are intellectual barriers as well."[22] William Birenbaum, a nationally prominent critic of American higher education who held administrative positions in several urban universities, wrote that in the modern city, "the idea of 'campus' is archaic. . . . The wide-open spaces, the monumental and inflexible architecture, and the insulation combine into an anti-urban phenomenon." He complained bitterly that "our colleges and universities have taken a very aloof position on the great urban issues."[23] Former University of California president Clark Kerr, a prominent analyst of American higher education, lamented that "today's urban universities are less involved in urban problems than they were in the 1930s. They are in the urban setting, but not of it."[24]

Several government officials criticized urban universities for neglecting the needs of cities. Detroit mayor Jerome Cavanagh, addressing the 1967 meeting of the AUU, admitted that urban universities "have made increasingly, even though at times it has been rather late, substantial contributions to the quality of life in the American city." However, he went on to say, "It is not enough, because the job has barely started."[25] Two years later, Boston mayor Kevin White wrote that with the rapid growth of urban problems, universities and cities had begun to pay attention to each other. The problems of cities, he argued, "have become so vast, so complex and so all-encompassing that the urban college has been virtually compelled to take notice."[26] Eldon Johnson, vice president of the University of Illinois, speaking at a 1974 ACE conference on urban universities, reported that large numbers of city and state officials disapproved of the unresponsiveness of research universities to city needs and the university's inability to do the kind of research that cities need.[27]

HUD leaders expressed similar criticisms. Joseph Coleman, deputy assistant secretary of HUD, stated, with regret, in 1968 that colleges and universities had not stood up to the challenge of American cities, and he warned that if they did not now do so, their importance to society would greatly diminish. Assistant secretary Charles Harr complained that the academic community showed "an inordinate aloofness that bars the full participation required to translate ideas into action." Few urban universities would receive high marks on their "willingness to engage in and with community issues."[28] At a conference of urban scholars in 1972, Assistant Secretary Samuel Jackson entitled his remarks "Is the University Superfluous in the Urban Crisis?" He answered "no" but complained that many academicians thought it inappropriate to get involved directly in city problems.[29] Likewise, Leonard Duhl, special assistant to the secretary of HUD, stated bluntly that "in influencing social policy in the cities or in being useful to mayors and city organizations or to Federal officials, on the whole the universities are bankrupt."[30]

Not surprisingly, the *New York Times* ran articles on universities' failure to address urban problems. A 1966 news story reported that the University of Minnesota, like other large universities across the country, was "taking a hard look at its commitment toward improving urban life." It indicated that many of the school's social science faculty opposed "the university's hands-off approach." An op-ed writer complained a few months later that "the urban university has failed to come to terms with the city in which it finds itself, has failed to plan its place in the urban environment over the long term, and has not linked up with the people of the community."[31]

Some argued that addressing the problems of the city, however important, distracted universities from their core mission of advancing and disseminating knowledge. The introduction to the summary of Boston University Metrocenter's third conference, devoted to "university and community action," stated that most university faculty members "are sympathetic to the cause of minority groups" but "are not sure that universities, including urban universities, should get into community action in a direct way." Instead they should undertake "independent, uncommitted research and teaching."[32] An Emory University philosopher of law and religion, Glenn Tinder, in a 1967 journal article, wrote that both universities and cities suffered from the decline of human civility. He concluded that universities must show responsibility to the city, not by "giving up study for action" but by "studying the philosophical truths and the social forms through which we enter the company of one another."[33] The dean of the Graduate School of Education at the University of Chicago articulated a more moderate position, arguing that universities should not embrace "isolation" but should also not engage in "direct social action." Scholars must "deal with reality," but they also need "some protection from daily action programs."[34]

Within urban universities, faculty and academic administrators also expressed significant reservations about the demands being put on them. In 1969, education scholar Colin Greer, associate editor of *Change Magazine*, wrote that universities should foster an environment "in which its collegiate family can *serve* rather than *use* its urban clientele." However, he expressed deep reservations about calls for an institution to "fundamentally change its traditional educative missions and to immerse itself totally in the service of the floundering urban core."[35] At the 1970 ACE conference, Cleveland State University president Harold Enarson gave numerous examples of universities' activities to address the problems of urban America. However, he urged universities to exercise extreme caution in undertaking too many initiatives, pointing to the lack of university funds and the impossibility of university service programs being able to "reverse the downward spiral of physical and human decay" in the ghetto.[36] In a similar vein, University of Cincinnati president Warren Bennis, writing in an ACE publication four years later, argued that the complexity of city problems defied resolution. He urged institutions to select carefully programs to address specific city problems that build on the university's research and teaching mission. But he warned that "any university could quickly exhaust even a hundred times its present resources by trying to solve—on its own—any single one of the problems" confronting the inner city.[37]

A decade later, Malcolm Moos assessed the urban outreach centers of universities in cities for the Ford Foundation. He noted significant variation in faculty attitudes from one institution to another. At the University of Wisconsin–Milwaukee, many professors participated in the city's civic life with wide acceptance from other faculty. Undoubtedly this resulted from the efforts of President J. Martin Klotsche to build the university as a distinctly urban institution. Faculty at the new Chicago Circle campus of the University of Illinois, by contrast, perceived service to the local community as having low status. Liberal arts faculty, who aspired to achieve the same national status as the flagship campus in Urbana, expressed especially strong opposition to community engagement. They "do not want to get their hands dirty," Moos observed, relating that faculty critical of community engagement argued that outreach activities "should have been managed through traditional disciplines instead of through newly created urban centers."[38] As late as 1980, a professor at the University of Wisconsin–Milwaukee noted unhappily that "many faculty members in today's urban universities are either confused about an 'urban mission' or are outright hostile to it" and "outreach efforts are resented for weakening the structure of the ivory tower."[39]

Defining the Urban University

Amid this intense discussion about the implications of the urban crisis for higher education, the dialogue on how to define the term "urban university" continued unabated. Nearly all commentators agreed that an institution located in a city should not automatically be classified as an "urban university." In his introduction to the proceedings of the 1963 AUU meeting, Martin Klotsche explained that the "term 'urban university' has never been satisfactorily defined" but stated nonetheless that it must be located in a large city and take responsibility for solving some of the city's problems.[40] In 1968, he told AUU attendees that their institutions' location in a city did not in itself make them urban universities. The urban university was "the primary institution in our society dedicated to the advancement of learning and the use of knowledge for the improvement of our society" because it addressed "the crises in our cities that confront this nation today."[41] A few months later, James Coleman addressed a national conference on universities and community service at the University of Maryland, telling his audience that higher education institutions in cities must clearly define their purpose. That purpose should be to educate professionals so they could address urban problems, undertake research on the problems of cities, provide service to their respective communities, develop a multidisciplinary approach to "identifying, analyzing and solving the complex physical and social problems of the urban community," and provide "the general civilizing quality of a liberal education" needed to live productively in an urban society."[42]

In 1970, Leonard Goodell, vice chancellor of the University of Illinois at Chicago Circle published an article in the *Journal of Higher Education* entitled "The Urban University: Is There Such a Thing?" He answered this question affirmatively and put forward a familiar list of urban university characteristics. To be an urban university, rather than just a university built in the city, an institution must undertake high-quality teaching, service, and research like other high-quality universities, but it must place much greater emphasis on community involvement and public service and take advantage of its city location to enrich teaching and research.[43]

This discussion of what it meant to be an urban university continued through the 1970s. Texas Southern University in Houston, one of the few historically black colleges located in a major city, emphatically defined itself as an "urban university" in the early 1970s. It president, Granville Sawyer, believed that Texas Southern needed a new mission, since other state institutions had begun to integrate racially, minimizing its traditional purpose of making higher education available to African Americans. The new mission, he argued, should be a university uniquely committed to addressing urban issues. The *Houston Post* endorsed this idea, stating in an editorial that Texas Southern should become an "urban university" because "it is located in the center of the nation's sixth largest city and in the heart of one of the City's largest black ghettoes, across the street from its oldest public housing project." In 1973, Sawyer got the state legislature to designate Texas Southern "as a special purpose institution of higher education for urban programming" and to mandate that it "provide instruction, research, programs, and services that are appropriate to this designation."[44]

In 1978, Maurice Berube published still another book on the urban university, arguing that its purpose must be to relate to "the wide range of issues faced by cities and their communities" and that it must be available to "everyone in the city."[45] A 1980 article in *Urban Education*, "Toward a Definition of an Urban University," insisted that it must respond directly to "the special needs of its community."[46]

Given this discussion, it is not surprising that many people insisted that an urban university must educate large numbers of local city residents. Some AUU institutional members enrolled relatively few local students. John Millett, former chancellor of the Ohio Board of Regents, told those attending the 1972 AUU meeting that a good number of universities located in cities are not "of the urban community." He specifically identified Harvard, MIT, Brown, Columbia, and the University of Chicago.[47] When the Ford Foundation initiated a program of grants in urban higher education in 1978, it required eligible institutions to be committed to educating primarily local residents.[48]

Some leaders of selective universities in cities reacted somewhat defensively to their low enrollment of local students. Under the leadership of James Hester, New York University, whose downtown campus for much of its history had served as a commuter institution for working New Yorkers, significantly raised its admission standards and recruited nationally. By 1971, about two-thirds of its students came from outside New York City. In a 1971 address, Hester insisted that NYU provided extensive services to the city and that his dominant objective was "to enhance our capacities as an urban university."[49]

Given the long-standing view that urban and commuter students lacked character and social refinement, the argument that urban universities had to serve large numbers of local students reinforced the idea that these institutions had low status. Before the 1960s, critics thought that their students' poor character and social refinement derived from their immigrant families and neighborhoods. Now, however, the image of urban students increasingly evoked black and Hispanic students from dysfunctional ghetto neighborhoods.

Explaining his goal in writing his book on universities and cities, Martin Klotsche acknowledged that "the identification of a university as urban has often been taken as a heavy handicap."[50] A staff member of the Ford Foundation, in a memo urging the extension of the foundation's education program to urban universities, argued that urban universities differed from "the great national universities which happen to be located in cities," like the University of Chicago and Harvard. The urban university "can be distinguished negatively by its relative lack of concern with being a 'national' university and positively by the closeness of its ties to the city and its problems."[51] A professor at the University of Louisville acknowledged in a 1980 journal article that "the adjective *urban* as a modifier for *university* conjures up distasteful thoughts in the minds of some faculty members, alumni, and university friends."[52]

Open Access

As discussions of what defined an urban university and how higher education should address the urban crisis raged, university departments, schools, centers, and individual faculty engaged in a wide range of activities in their host cities. Many institutions changed their admissions practices and developed affirmative action programs to increase the number of minority and local students. "Open admissions" or "open enrollment" programs, which allowed any high school graduate to enroll in a public four-year institution, generated widespread discussion.

The City University of New York (CUNY) faced by far the most intense public controversy over special programs to increase minority enrollment. In the early 1960s, black students constituted only 2 percent of the enrollment of CUNY's oldest and most esteemed institution, City College of New York (CCNY), located in Harlem, a neighborhood often seen as the center of black political and cultural life. In 1963, City College initiated a pilot program, College Discovery, which allowed a principal or guidance counselor to select two graduates from low-income families whose grades fell below the minimum required for admission to attend CUNY. Two years later, CUNY expanded this CCNY program, selecting 150 black high school graduates from Harlem and the Bronx with an insufficient grade average and provided them with remediation and counseling to prepare them for regular college courses. Students who succeeded in elevating their academic skills could then enroll in City College's baccalaureate program. In 1966, CUNY's chancellor changed the name of the program to Search for Education, Elevation and Knowledge (SEEK). The following year, the state legislature extended SEEK to all of CUNY. A few years later, the City University system established the One Hundred Scholars program, guaranteeing admission to the top hundred graduates of every New York City high school.

In August 1968, following the assassination of Martin Luther King and the civil disturbances that followed, the New York Board of Higher Education asked the City University chancellor to report on progress in getting "minority groups represented in the units of the University in the same proportion as they are represented among all high school graduates in the City." The preamble to this resolution explained the urgency of having "high school graduates from economically deprived neighborhoods and homes . . . provided with equalized opportunity for post-high school education."[53]

In 1969, African American and Puerto Rican students engaged in a campus sit-in, demanding, among other things, that the racial composition of the college's entering class equal the proportion of all New York City high school graduates, meaning that approximately 40 percent of new students would have to be African American or Puerto Rican. In response to these protests and to political pressure from civil rights activists, in May 1969 CUNY announced a dual-admissions system in which half the entering student body would be selected following traditional academic criteria and the other half from designated high schools in low-income neighborhoods. The plan aroused vigorous objections, and the board soon withdrew it.

In its place, the Board of Higher Education voted that, effective 1970, every high school graduate would be ensured admission to one of the CUNY campuses, which included several two-year community colleges. This did not, however, guarantee all students admission to a particular four-year college or to any four-year college. Students whose academic grades averaged 80 or above in high school courses, or who graduated in the top half of their class, would be admitted to one of the four-year schools. Other students would be admitted if space was available. The new admissions process eliminated use of the SAT and also abolished the requirement that applicants needed to complete a minimum number of academic courses in English, math, foreign language, and science to be eligible for admission to a senior college. Students graduating from vocational or commercial high schools would be treated the same as those from academic high schools.[54] Although public discussion of minority enrollment focused on admissions processes and requirements, advocates of open access also insisted that colleges establish substantial academic support and tutoring programs for less-well-prepared students.

As a result, the number of SEEK students at City College almost tripled between 1969 and 1970, to two thousand, and the number of non-SEEK minority students tripled to 15 percent of City College enrollment. A year later, black students, not including those in SEEK, made up 19 percent of City College enrollment and Puerto Rican students 7 percent. By 1977, that representation grew to 31 percent black and 16 percent Puerto Rican. Many working-class whites, mostly children or grandchildren of European immigrants, also benefited from the new admissions standards.[55]

Although colleges in many other cities instituted similar programs, the initiative at City University, and especially at City College, received the most public attention. City College in the years before and after World War II had an overwhelmingly Jewish student body, mostly from working-class backgrounds. In the prewar era, there were almost no Jewish faculty, but from the 1950s, a growing number of City College alumni held faculty positions at City College and many other universities.[56] While most of these faculty supported civil rights and the need to increase black and Puerto Rican enrollment, some, as well as many other Jewish alumni, saw open admission as dramatically undermining the rigorous academic standards that they remembered.

Vast numbers of articles and several books assessed the impact of open access. Proponents cited the rapidly growing percentage of minority students enrolled at City University and CCNY, arguing that the enlarged college enrollment of low-income and minority students would address, in part, the urban crisis. The American system of higher education, they maintained, had historically provided opportunity primarily for socially and economically advantaged students.[57] A City College English professor wrote that open admissions students "can draw upon experiences that are unusual in the classroom and exceedingly valuable, thereby enhancing the educational experiences of all students."[58] Leonard Kriegel, a prominent and prolific writer who taught at City College, published a book in 1972 on "a teacher's journey in the urban university." Acknowledging that open admission created significant problems for CCNY, he nonetheless hoped that it would promote the democratic ideal that education should be open to all and would "turn the college into an urban model for the nation."[59] Irving Howe, an English professor at Hunter College, argued that " 'equality of opportunity is impossible when the circumstances of competing groups are so different': the culture of poor blacks shaped by years of blatant discrimination made it very difficult for black high school graduates to compete with graduates from other groups."[60]

Critics of open admission often pointed to the high attrition rate of students who would not have been admitted under traditional standards. Before open enrollment, about 18 percent of first-year students dropped out. After the first year of open enrollment, the drop-out rate rose to 35 percent. One CUNY professor published a journal article arguing that this high rate of attrition stemmed from the "difficulties of adjustment from ghetto life and schooling to the university, the social and economic demands of their own families" and the high rate of unemployment among minorities, which called into question their "ability to obtain a position, even with a college degree."[61] In a similar vein, journalist Martin Mayer wrote in 1973 that a considerable majority of open enrollment students who did not drop out performed badly, explaining that most of them were "dull students" for whom college constituted "the forced prolongation of an outworn adolescence for purposes that are quite separate from the civilizing Idea of a university."[62]

Opponents of open enrollment most often said that it greatly lowered the quality of education at what had been an elite institution in academic quality if not in social status. Harvard sociologist and City College alumnus Nathan Glazer—in an article entitled "Are Academic Standards Obsolete?"—expressed concern that universities now placed diminished importance on the intellectual ability of students. "In the past," he wrote, "the practices that substituted class and ethnic criteria for academic ability were criticized because they served to keep down the poor and the ethnic. . . . [I]t was the American Jews, suffering most from such practices, who launched the most powerful attack on the use of any criteria but tested academic ability."[63] City College's dean of humanities expressed exasperation that faculty "trained to preserve the best that has been thought and said" now had "to teach Shakespeare to a student who two years earlier had been struggling to compose coherent sentences." The minority students at City College, he complained, "came from working-class families in which television and radio were the exclusive sources of information and in which there was no tradition of learning."[64]

San Francisco State University changed its admissions policies for minority students after a dramatic five-month student strike, the longest strike in the history of American higher education. The student protests began with sit-ins and other demonstrations demanding that the university give students a much larger role in institutional governance, that it combat racism, and that it not reveal student academic standing to the Selective Service, thereby supporting the draft and the Vietnam War. When the administration suspended George Murray, a graduate student in English and Minister of Education for the militant Black Panther Party, the Black Student Union united with the Third World Liberation Front, a coalition of Latin American, Filipino, and Mexican

Strike poster, San Francisco State University, 1968. SF State Strike Collection, University Archives, San Francisco State University.

student organizations, demanding expansion of the Black Studies department, the creation of a School of Ethnic Studies, and increased recruitment and admission of minority students. After a week of conflict between protesting students and San Francisco police, the president closed the university and resigned not long thereafter.

The campus faculty union then joined the strike, supporting many of the student demands and seeking a decrease in faculty workload. After several months, the university administration reached an agreement with both the faculty union and the students. Although the university already had a special admissions program for black and other minority students, as a result of the strike it vastly increased its recruitment of nonwhite students and greatly increased the number of special admissions students with weaker academic records. It also enlarged the Black Studies department and established a School of Ethnic Studies.

Open enrollment at City College proved vastly more contentious than in other places. However, many other institutions admitted students irrespective of their high school record. The University of Kansas, Wyoming, Arkansas, and Alaska, as well as Ohio State and Montana State, accepted all high school graduates, but none of these had significant enrollment of minority students from big cities. Rutgers University announced in 1969 that it would automatically admit graduates from high schools in Newark, New Brunswick, and Camden to the Rutgers campuses located in their respective cities and establish special support programs for these students. Federal City College (now the University of the District of Columbia), opened in 1968 in Washington, DC, a majority black city that until then had no public higher education other than a teachers college. It embraced open admission from its inception. And numerous two-year junior and community colleges also admitted all high school graduates.[65]

In 1972, the New York State Regents adopted a policy calling for increased minority access to higher education. It asked every postsecondary institution in the state to prepare a comprehensive plan to expand the enrollment of minority students and the numbers of minority faculty. It also called on each institution to develop a plan to sensitize faculty, staff, and students to "the diverse life-styles of the increasing number of minority group students being admitted."[66] Not surprisingly, the demands of the civil rights movement in the mid-1960s to increase minority presence in colleges and universities had its greatest impact on institutions in cities with large minority populations.

Efforts to Improve City Government

The long-standing effort by universities to improve the quality of city government workers through education in public administration continued during the urban crisis. But now universities emphasized direct assistance to city governments through applied research and training programs. In 1963, the University of Chicago launched a program for mayors, municipal council members, and planning commissioners to teach them about current urban planning research and its application the contemporary city.[67] Florida State University's Urban Research Center ran a program in the mid-1960s for public administrators, mayors, county and city commissioners, fire chiefs, businessmen, and educators, designed to help them "identify and alleviate community problems."[68]

At the University of Pennsylvania, the Fels Institute of Local and State Government continued to provide university courses for full-time graduate students planning to work in city government and for elected or appointed city officials, as well as one-day conferences for officials on the problems and functions of government. Fels also conducted a consulting service for local and state governments on a wide range of issues. It ran Community Leadership seminars to get representatives of industry in the Philadelphia area involved in community issues. Also, the University of Pennsylvania's Center for Urban Research and Experiment undertook a project to develop strategies to deal with urban racial problems by bringing together policy makers and social scientists in a year-long dialogue.[69]

In the mid-1970s, the University of Cincinnati secured funding to develop a capacity-building program for the city council, focused on teaching council members to secure and analyze data needed for decision making. It then collaborated with the University of Dayton in a series of workshops in public sector labor-management relations for managers in cities, counties, and public school systems.[70] In Detroit, Wayne State University and the University of Michigan created the Detroit City/University Consortium in 1977 to consult with city officials, analyze policy options, and undertake "mini-research" projects.[71]

Some public administration faculty argued that city governments had to adapt to rapidly changing technology that could significantly improve the governance of cities. In 1967, the Fels Institute and the American Academy of Political and Social Science published an analysis of how science and technology affected local government. One scholar, writing about the computer and the urban revolution, predicted that by 1990 "the principal public utility will be a gigantic communications network . . . of huge computers." Two years later, a committee of the National Academy of Sciences and the National Academy of Engineering prepared a report, commissioned by HUD, addressing how this federal department should develop its research capacity. In 1974, the American Council on Education's urban affairs office ran a course on linking technology to urban management, undoubtedly assuming that university personnel would convey what they learned to their respective city governments.[72]

Adult Education

Although adult education providers had an enduring connection to urban universities, the urban crisis caused many universities in cities, government agencies, and foundations to make part-time education for working adults a higher priority. Writing in 1975, a faculty member at the University of Missouri argued that "the new urban consciousness" had caused faculty in institutions located in cities to accept higher adult education because "the concept of urban is related directly to existing social conditions."[73] Advocates of adult education argued that it provided opportunities for city residents to get better jobs and improve their economic status. They also asserted that it would enhance the civic consciousness of city dwellers and give them the knowledge they needed to improve social conditions in their communities.

Promoters of adult education drew an analogy between the historic work of land-grant cooperative extension programs and the need for urban extension programs in cities.[74] The concept of urban extension encompassed much more than the various forms of adult education, but for many universities the term meant providing education to a wide range of city residents.

The University of Wisconsin extension program trained inner-city Milwaukee residents for jobs as homemakers or hospital aides, taught unemployed people how to secure a new job, and helped local residents to pass civil service exams. It also offered courses on how to care for aging people and a health education program for expectant and new mothers. Still other programs sought to educate inner city people about credit traps, wise buying, and food stamps. It also sponsored a business management course for inner-city African American businessmen.[75]

Rutgers University's Urban Studies Center provided instruction to poor women in Newark on meal preparation, housekeeping, and "economical shopping methods." It offered programs to help teachers use techniques that would be effective with inner-city youth and human relations courses for police.

Boston University expanded the adult education programs of Metrocenter in 1966 into Metropolitan College. In addition to a range of extension courses already offered to city residents, it began baccalaureate degree programs in liberal studies and applied science for students whose education had been interrupted for economic or personal reasons, as well as programs for teachers and nurses.[76]

Wayne State University opened a Weekend College for adults in 1973, based on the premise that "in today's world all must have access to higher education." The program organizers designed it to meet the needs of working adult students, whose experiences, they argued, differed substantially from just-out-of-high-school students. They hoped to draw on adult students' extensive life experiences and decided that each academic quarter would have a different interdisciplinary focus, among them ethnic studies, work and labor, the quality of life, the performing arts, and science and energy. The Weekend College developed a close relationship with the United Automobile Workers union, and its leaders bragged that the factory worker had become "a prototype of the working adult student for whom the weekend college concept was designed."[77]

Many private universities also undertook extension programs, not only to enable local residents to get degrees that would help them advance economically but also to educate local community citizens and their leaders on the nature of the social problems they confronted in their neighborhoods. For example, NYU's School of Continuing Education conducted discussion groups in Harlem on "child development, consumer awareness, educational problems, and Negro history in order to extend non-credit adult education programs to poor neighborhoods.[78] Syracuse University established what it called the Thursday Morning Round Table, a discussion of social problems with sixty-five local civic leaders and citizens. Twice a year, it also hosted a two-day retreat devoted to a specific local issue.[79] Northwestern University's Center for Urban Affairs provided funding to four Chicago civic organizations so that they could engage researchers to study and therefore improve these groups' work in the city.[80] The University of Pennsylvania ran a summer program for unemployed male high school dropouts, and a six-week program to help low-income high school graduates who had been admitted to college prepare for the transition.[81]

Despite the proliferation of these and many other urban extension programs, some higher educators articulated concerns about the problems faced by inner-city working adults, not unlike those expressed by others about open enrollment students. A 1976 article in the *Journal of Higher Education* noted that "up to sixty percent of urban populations may suffer from at least moderately severe emotional trouble."[82] And an essay published by two professors in 1980 argued that adult educators in the inner city faced students who wanted to "perpetuate their ethnicity owing to the security and reinforcement it brings them," thereby isolating themselves from their middle-class instructors. They also said that instructors faced students with "low self-image" created by their lack of success.[83]

Using the City for Teaching

From the beginning of the twentieth century, advocates of urban universities argued that cities provided rich opportunities for student learning. In 1906, the engineering program at the University of Cincinnati initiated its cooperative learning program. By 1920 ten universities offered cooperative learning programs; that number grew to sixty-one by 1960. As the urban crisis caused more and more institutions to teach students about the inner city and to provide service to ghetto communities, the number of cooperative education programs grew to about 225 in 1971 and 600 in 1973. Scholars of higher education estimated that eighty thousand students participated in a cooperative education program in 1974.[84]

The rapid growth of programs engaging urban college students with their cities went way beyond cooperative education. Internships, research projects, and what later would be called "service-learning" initiatives spread throughout much of higher education, with universities in cities leading the way. In 1961, Howard University created a Community Service Project, which gave students, primarily in sociology and anthropology, "experience in surveying an area of social disorganization" to give them "first-hand experience with neighborhood problems and experience with social science methods."[85] The University of Southern California offered an Urban Semester program in which students devoted the entire semester to research on social problems in Los Angeles and the study of urban affairs. The class met at different locations in the city, but not on campus. Later, it inaugurated a program in which students received academic credit for service to public schools in the low-income and largely minority neighborhood surrounding the campus. They taught mini-courses on subjects related to their own academic program, served as tutors and teachers' aides, and assisted with parent education.[86]

A 1967 University of Pennsylvania review of student-community involvement reported that 330 students tutored city youth and 200 students volunteered with organizations concerned with juvenile delinquency, prisons, social work, and "mental and general hospitals." Columbia University created a Citizenship Program in which baccalaureate student volunteers tutored "underprivileged" children, assisted hospital personnel in low-income neighborhoods, and worked in government offices. They did not receive academic credit for these activities.[87]

As student activism grew in the wake of the civil rights movement, student organizations also created programs to serve low-income communities near their campuses. The National Student Association created a Community Action Curriculum to "encourage and aid colleges and universities to initiate curricular programs in community action" for which students would receive academic credit.[88]

Champions of student community engagement had long argued that it strengthened learning and better prepared students for civic responsibilities. A professor at the University of California, Berkeley, for example, insisted that to educate leaders capable of developing solutions to the problems faced by cities, universities would need to recognize that "the best teaching and the best learning occur in the course of laboratory-like experimentation in problem solving" relevant to "the lives of real people in real cities."[89] Others strongly objected to the idea of experimentation. A businessman who served as a University of Wisconsin trustee, speaking at an ACE conference in 1970, acknowledged that while cities offered excellent opportunities to combine practice and learning, universities should not "experiment on the populace" surrounding the university.[90] Elden Jacobson, a researcher at the Washington Center for Metropolitan Studies, argued against urban internships because students are then "schooled by the very institutions that account for much of our present social malaise." Moreover, it placed them "in roles vis-à-vis the city that they are very unlikely to occupy again," because most of them come from the suburbs and will return to the suburbs.[91]

Research on Cities

Not surprisingly, with growing public focus on the urban crisis, many universities established urban research centers. A directory of these centers, published in 1969, stated that their number had grown from eighty in 1967 to approximately two hundred by 1969. Many scholars studying urban issues insisted that this research could lead to mitigation of city problems. An introduction to the 1969 directory, for example, declared enthusiastically that "this growth represents a problem-solving potential of considerable magnitude."[92] The federal government also greatly expanded its urban research and data collection. In

1968, President Johnson created the Urban Institute as a nonprofit organization devoted to research on the effectiveness of government programs addressing urban problems.[93]

Some social scientists studying cities, however, argued that current urban research could not solve city problems. One speaker at a 1967 conference on college-community consultation argued that to date urban social scientists had not learned "how to correlate their insights" to find solutions to "the human problems of urban life."[94] Two years later, a political scientist and dean at Syracuse University told attendees of a conference at Boston University that universities were being called on "with embarrassing frequency to recommend solutions to baffling community issues," asserting that scholars "lack the tools at the moment even to find out how to begin the process of analysis . . . which ultimately might lead to useful knowledge."[95] The following year, a report of a Harvard committee on the university and the city concluded that the major problems of society "are not ones that will yield readily, if at all, to the kinds of knowledge university intellectuals can produce."[96] At roughly the same time, William Gorham, a former assistant secretary at HUD and director of a new federally sponsored urban institute, told attendees at a National Association of State Universities and Land-Grant Colleges (NASULGC) meeting that most university urban research institutes had failed to contribute to solving city problems.[97] The Ford Foundation, which had funded much of this research, undertook an assessment of its urban program in 1976. The report concluded that "strikingly little of the advice generated by academics had the intended effect, or indeed any effect, on cities" at least partly because city governments "had limited capacity to act on recommendations for change."[98]

Others reiterated the concern that attempts to solve city problems distracted universities from their core mission of teaching and research. Warren Bennis, president of the University of Cincinnati, warned readers of the *Educational Record* that "any university could quickly exhaust even a hundred times its present resources by trying to solve" any one of the major urban problems "on its own." He agreed that universities in cities should help to ameliorate one or more specific problems that drew on the institution's special strengths. "Better to do one important small job well than to fail at a dozen big ones," he wrote.[99]

Views of Urban Students

Not surprisingly, given the great expansion of access to college and the rapid growth of commuter students, the ongoing discussions about the problems of urban students, begun around the time of the establishment of AUU in 1914, continued throughout the urban crisis and beyond. College and university leaders still talked about the important role higher education played in building character in students. Now, however, they meant building social and civic responsibility, respect for different cultural backgrounds and religions, and the ability to communicate effectively with a wide range of people.

The proportion of college students in the United States aged nineteen or twenty who lived at home with one or two parents rose from 35 percent in 1960 to 47 percent by 1980. Most of these commuter students came from middle-class homes, taking advantage of the great increase in local institutions that had not been available to students of a similar background twenty years earlier.[100] Despite this fact, however, higher education leaders still believed that they had a special responsibility to focus on character development among commuter students, and in particular on the social and cultural problems of the "disadvantaged," particularly of African American "ghetto students."

In *The Urban University and the Future of Our Cities*, published in 1966, Martin Klotsche acknowledged that urban commuter students were often "slow to break away from high school habits" and had parents who "hover protectively over their children." Therefore, this kind of student "is inclined to view his education narrowly."[101] A 1970 report on commuter students at Wayne State University reported that family members "make demands of time and energy which devour much of the spiritual reserve of urban students."[102] An essay by two staff members of Northeastern Illinois University in Chicago asserted that "urban commuter institutions have a perennial problem" of "building a sense of community."[103]

A good number of faculty articulated similar concerns about the inadequacy of urban commuter students. The distinguished sociologist David Riesman noted unhappily in 1967 that urban commuter students "go home again to their uncomprehending families and their non-college friends" where they are "surrounded by people who think liberal education is merely another kind of trade school."[104] Three other sociologists writing in 1970 predicted that "college education in the city may become something less central, less engrossing and less of a discernible life-cycle stage than we have come to think of it as represented in the traditional residential colleges."[105]

Mental health professionals and student counselors shared these views, as well as other concerns about commuters. A psychiatric social worker at the University of Illinois Chicago Circle campus complained in 1966 that the

"Polish, Lithuanian, Jewish, Negro, Greek, Italian, Mexican, Ukrainian, and other groups" from the ghetto who attended his institution had "to a large extent . . . kept their faces turned inward and toward the past." The working-class commuter student "steps into a world that is most unfamiliar, and may return each afternoon to a home that is antagonized by his physical and ideological departure."[106] The following year, the dean of California State University, Long Beach wrote in the *Journal of the American College Health Association* about psychological problems afflicting commuter students, "characterized by apathy, depression, lack of affective reaction, and concomitant identity crisis [with] some of the characteristics of the schizoid personality." Urging colleges to do whatever they could to keep students on the campus and have them participate in campus activities, he asserted, "The blight of anonymity is, without question, one of the foremost problems on the large, impersonal campus of most metropolitan colleges."[107] And in 1974, Thomas Harrington, in his book *Student Personnel Work in Urban Colleges*, repeated the familiar litany of urban commuter student problems. These students "find it difficult to . . . understand the new behaviors expected of them or to meet the college faculty's expectation for self-direction." Moreover, "they must still relate daily with their siblings and parents" who may have no tolerance for "newer values that they learn in college" that might conflict with the family's social, religious, and political views.[108] Harrington's observations reiterated concerns about the negative influence of immigrant families and neighborhoods on adult students.

Scholars of higher education supported this view of commuters. A psychiatrist writing in 1964 hypothesized that separation from home constituted a normal developmental stage for young people and that many students who selected nonresidential colleges did so because of mental health problems.[109] In 1965, a faculty member at the University of Minnesota presented the results of a study he undertook comparing resident and nonresident students at a large Midwestern university, concluding that "commuters had a significantly greater number of problems" than residence hall students did. The resident students had substantially better vocabulary, whereas the commuter students had greater problems in their finances, living conditions, employment, home, and family.[110] A study comparing resident and commuter students at a private liberal arts college in an eastern city, published in 1970, surmised that "the commuter students had poorer mental health and curricular adjustment and showed less maturity of goals and aspiration than resident students."[111] An article on a study of St. Louis area high school graduates confirmed the widely held view that students from higher socioeconomic backgrounds chose residential colleges in much greater numbers than low-income and working-class students. However, it found "different manifest personality needs" between these two groups. Commuter students sought "autonomy and dominance," while resident students felt a need for change and the desire to be more aggressive.[112]

The civil rights movement and the racial disturbances in cities in the late 1960s put great pressure on universities, especially those in cities, to significantly increase their enrollment of black and Hispanic students. At the same time, educators and policy makers wrote extensively about the need for "universal higher education," arguing that extending access to education from high school to college was a natural extension of American tradition at a time when more and more jobs required a college degree.[113] Two-year junior colleges had been a modest part of higher education in the prewar era; now called community colleges, they proliferated and greatly expanded their enrollments, as did public four-year institutions. A modest number of African American students, mostly from middle-class homes, had attended college since the mid-nineteenth century. They had enrolled primarily in historically black institutions, located mostly in the South. But after World War II, as many African Americans relocated from the South to northern cities, increasing numbers of black students enrolled in public institutions to which they could commute. Now, as politicians, policy makers, and educators debated open enrollment and access to higher education, they focused ever more sharply on "urban students."

University leaders now described these low-income black and Hispanic students as academically and culturally "disadvantaged." Unlike their predecessors, they did not complain about these students' lack of social refinement. Indeed, a growing number of faculty had themselves commuted to college from working-class neighborhoods, the very students earlier generations of faculty found lacking in character and social skills. Instead, they complained about academic preparedness, motivation, and personal discipline.

Although university leaders rarely if ever publicly expressed hostility to these disadvantaged students, they talked a good deal about the students' problems and about what institutions needed to do to address these. They also expressed growing concern about students' poor academic preparation and their inability to meet academic expectations. Martin Klotsche wrote in 1966 that universities must "face up to facts about disadvantaged youth that do not apply to other segments of our society." Because the "family environment among Negroes is often disruptive," university personnel must gain "an understanding of the structure and functioning of the Negro family."[114] In the same year, Earl McGrath, former US commissioner of education and a professor at Teachers College, wrote that to establish higher educational opportunity for all, colleges and universities would need to induce in disadvantaged inner-city students "motivation and aspiration . . . to avoid their otherwise certain candidacy for early dropout." He urged that methods be found "to compensate for the educational deprivation which the environment of home and school have added to their other woes."[115] City College president Robert Marshak expressed pride in the large increase of black, Puerto Rican, and low-income students attending his institution as a result of open enrollment. However, he acknowledged that it had created a "large admixture of academically underprepared students entering the College" and that "the challenge of serving the urban community is filled with problems and frustrations."[116]

In 1970, the American College Testing Program published *The Ghetto College Student.* Arguing that the problems of ghetto students differed from those of all other students from working-class and disadvantaged groups, the author, sociologist Gordon D. Morgan, explained that the ghetto child "receives little guidance from home" and "spends his time discovering ways to work outside the system instead of working within it." The ghetto college student, he said, is suspicious of all white people, "and his inability to be hurt by a failing grade serves to disarm the traditional teacher."[117] A 1973 study of students in a California equal-opportunity program concluded that universities needed to help disadvantaged students improve their "self-concept," noting that "the smooth transition from a ghetto (from which most disadvantaged students matriculate) to the liberal arts college environment is a difficult task."[118]

The "urban crisis" had a profound effect on American higher education. It brought about significant enrollment growth, advancing the role of urban public universities in expanding the democratization of America's higher education system. This, in turn, extended higher education's traditional goal of character building, which shifted its priority to civic responsibility, and especially toward addressing the cultural deficiencies of ghetto residents.

The "urban crisis" also focused public attention on the role that universities could play in addressing economic inequality, racism, and the needs of cities and their residents. Universities in cities greatly increased research and academic programs in urban studies. In expanding their service to cities, they advanced a commitment to community service and experiential learning in institutions across the country. Elite universities in cities joined in providing services to their communities, undertook more urban research, and used their expertise to address some of the needs of their communities. However, they had only a marginal role in meeting the demand for lower-income and minority access to higher education.

These efforts by universities to mitigate the social ills of cities further reinforced the idea that term "urban university" first and foremost referred to institutions that enrolled large numbers of local commuter students. As a result, "urban university" became a low-status label, which many universities in cities now avoided. Not surprisingly, the Association of Urban Universities voted itself out of existence in 1977, reflecting the resistance of its members to the term "urban university." Although universities in cities had led the nation in democratization of higher education, the image of many urban public institutions declined due to racism and anti-urbanism, now focused on city slums and ghettos.

5

Government, Universities, and the Urban Crisis, 1964–1980

Given the depth of problems faced by cities during the "urban crisis," it is hardly surprising that federal, state, and local governments looked to universities in cities as agents capable of addressing some of these issues. Civic, government, and community leaders since the early twentieth century had urged urban higher educational institutions to address these problems. Now, however, government developed extensive programs to address the severe poverty and racial inequality in cities.

President Lyndon Johnson, in his State of the Union address in January 1964, declared that his administration would undertake an "unconditional war on poverty." He got Congress to enact the Economic Opportunity Act, which created the Jobs Corps program for young low-income males and a new Office of Economic Opportunity and allocated substantial funds for antipoverty programs. He also secured passage of the Housing Act of 1964, providing funds for housing construction, renovation, and urban renewal, which he succeeded in greatly expanding the following year. The new federal Department of Housing and Urban Development was established as a cabinet department in 1965. In 1966, Johnson got Congress to fund a Model Cities program, providing federal funds to help cities facing "race riots."[1]

Many of these and other Johnson administration programs depended on universities or their faculties. Many scholars, particularly in the social sciences, welcomed the opportunity to participate in the "war on poverty" and "the great society." In 1965, Congress passed and Johnson signed a Higher Education Act providing extensive funding to universities as a means of addressing poverty. Speaking on the importance of this legislation, the president drew on the familiar land-grant analogy: "Just as our colleges and universities changed the future of our farms a century ago, so they can help change the future of our cities." The act authorized substantial federal funds to strengthen community service resources and continuing education.

A senior official of the Department of Education explained to delegates at the 1965 Association of Urban Universities meeting that the administration expected that the act would support studies of employment problems and economic growth, seminars for community leaders, conferences on extending health care, research in urban planning, radio and television programs aimed at uplifting the poor, and support for community groups to develop programs addressing these needs. The act also provided funds for university libraries, for "developing institutions," and for a variety of programs to assist lower-income students in financing college education. It created the Teacher Corps to get motivated college graduates to become teachers in low-income schools, and it provided grants to universities to improve preparation of teachers for schools whose students were mostly poor.[2]

In 1966, the newly established Model Cities program sought to coordinate the resources and programs of city, state, and federal government to mitigate urban ills in selected areas. George Arnstein, a HUD consultant, urged universities to address four key program needs: evaluating the effect of Model Cities on the selected areas, creating mechanisms for local citizen participation, training people living in the area to run the program, and providing technical and administrative assistance. Several universities provided important professional and technical support to their local Model Cities program.[3]

President Richard Nixon, who took office in January 1969, scaled back federal funding for urban programs but did not eliminate them. He argued for a "new federalism," reducing federal control over local policy. He secured legislation in 1974 that consolidated various federal urban programs, including urban renewal and Model Cities, into a single initiative, the Community Development Block Grant, which provided funds to cities with populations over 500,000.[4] Nixon's successors, Gerald Ford and Jimmy Carter, did not substantially increase federal urban funding and supported public-private partnerships to address the growing disinvestment in and population decline of cities.

The "new federalism" also called on universities to address city needs. In the late 1960s, HUD took a new approach to the long-standing effort to improve the quality of city government employees. In 1969, HUD awarded Urban Fellowships to ninety-nine students to prepare for work in government. Upon graduation, about 90 percent of the fellows went to work in urban-related professions, and 70 percent took jobs in government.[5] HUD also developed "University without Walls," sending faculty to offer instruction to working adults at their worksites or at other convenient locations and using a modern version of correspondence instruction, including lectures on cassettes, slides, videotapes, and movies.[6]

The US Office of Education joined in these efforts to have urban universities address the "urban crisis." In June 1970, it released a commissioned report entitled *Urban Universities: Rhetoric, Reality and Conflict*, intended to guide universities in cities in building partnerships with local government and with neighborhoods adjacent to their campuses. The report's researchers studied eleven higher education institutions in depth and provided a range of suggestions on how universities in cities could overcome the traditional barriers between them and local residents to begin to meet the serious social and economic needs of their communities. These suggestions included allocating a portion of the university's purchases to local enterprises, insisting that construction companies working on campus structures employ black workers, placing a priority on hiring local residents for university jobs, and opening some campus facilities for use by community residents.[7]

The Intergovernmental Personnel Act of 1970, administered by the Civil Service Commission, offered the opportunity for state and local government employees to return to graduate school as full-time students. It also made possible the assignment of local government employees to universities for a discrete period of time or for professors to be assigned temporarily to a city government agency. In 1971 and 1972, forty-seven different universities participated.[8]

Urban Observatories

Universities, and social scientists in particular, welcomed the expanding federal efforts to involve faculty in research on cities and the financial support provided to scholars of cities. In 1967, HUD engaged the National Academy of Sciences to prepare two reports on the status of urban research and how it might address the problems of the "urban crisis." A National Academy committee of distinguished social scientists wrote a report entitled *A Strategic Approach to Urban Research and Development: Social and Behavioral Science Considerations*. It acknowledged that city, state, and federal governments facing physical deterioration, poverty, and racial conflict in the cities "have been able to draw only to a limited extent upon the relatively small body of relevant social and behavioral knowledge." It argued boldly that attempts to address urban problems required knowledge of cities and urban life, arguing that "had the launching of urban programs been accompanied by the understanding that it is virtually as important to learn about the nation's cities as it is to do something for them, the cities might not be in their present plight." The committee's first recommendation called for university research on cities, noting that universities employed most of the nation's social and behavioral researchers and that "many of them are increasingly concerned with urban research."[9]

Social scientists convinced HUD to fund urban observatories, a major program supporting urban research at universities in cities. The push for funding began in 1962, when political scientist Robert Wood, then a professor at the Massachusetts Institute of Technology, spoke at a conference on urban life and form at Washington University in St. Louis. He suggested that social scientists who studied cities and urban issues were far behind natural scientists. Natural scientists, he argued, could use field stations, data centers, and observatories to collect information systematically. Wood proposed establishment of urban observatories that would undertake "a common series of investigations under a single research plan which for the first time would provide us with professionally reliable findings simultaneously in a number of areas." This would, in turn, provide a sound basis for the application of systematic knowledge about cities to public policy.[10]

About two years later, Milwaukee mayor Henry W. Maier read Wood's speech and embraced it as "a long-awaited dream of those of us on the municipal firing line." Maier, who served as president of the National League of Cities (NLC) in 1964–1965, called a meeting of twenty-three mayors and urban scholars from nineteen universities on June 3, 1965, in Milwaukee, to discuss Wood's idea. The mayors showed keen interest in applied research that could inform policy making. The academicians generally expressed interest in data gathering and pure research.

Nonetheless, the attendees unanimously adopted the "Milwaukee Resolve" requesting that the NLC "serve as an integrating and stimulating force" in the development of a network of urban observatories. Shortly thereafter, the NLC established a permanent standing committee on urban observatories, with Wood and Maier as co-chairs. In calling for federal funding for the urban observatories, Maier noted that "the Organic Act of 1862 . . . established the Department of Agriculture and charged it from the beginning with conducting an agricultural research program." He urged similar federal support for urban research.[11]

In January 1966, Robert Wood became undersecretary of the new US Department of Housing and Urban Development. On July 1, 1968, HUD contracted with the NLC to begin an urban observatory program. The NLC invited applications from 115 mayors, of whom fifty-six expressed interest. In evaluating the applicants, NLC looked for places where university scholars and government officials already worked together successfully and for universities that had a substantial track record of urban research. Initially, NLC selected six cities—Atlanta, Albuquerque, Baltimore, Kansas City, Milwaukee, and Nashville. In 1970, it added four others—Boston, San Diego, Cleveland, and Denver. The program required close collaboration between universities and city government. Funding came from both HUD and the Department of Education.[12]

Urban observatories in each city conducted a wide range of studies. The program required all observatories to study certain common issues in order to create a national database on matters of great importance to cities and to enable comparative research and deeper understanding of these problems. The common issues included a survey of citizen attitudes toward taxes and services, studies of citizen participation, municipal revenues and expenditures, indicators of urban social conditions and change, and the cost of providing services for substandard housing. Most observatories conducted other studies of specifically local issues as well. The Albuquerque observatory, for example, examined the city's emergency medical services, resulting in a new city ordinance on ambulances. The Boston observatory looked at the municipality's "Little City Halls," a study that provided an impetus for the mayor of Boston to strengthen this program. The San Diego, Denver, and Albuquerque observatories studied ways to revise their city charters.

University researchers at the observatories established working partnerships with city government officials, but those relationships sometimes experienced strain because government officials needed immediate answers and scholars viewed research and data collection as a necessarily extended enterprise. Urban observatories received considerable attention among academicians, some of whom saw them as a unique opportunity to connect social scientific research on cities to urban government decision making. In 1974, HUD decided that "because the Observatories had been successful," continued funding for them should now be obtained from local sources. Most observatories were able to find funding for a few years, but by the end of the decade the network of observatories had largely disappeared.[13]

The Urban Grant University

Even as the urban observatory program continued evolving, higher education leaders advocated a broader federal program of "urban grant universities." On October 18, 1967, Clark Kerr, director of the Carnegie Commission's study of higher education and immediate past-president of the University of California, addressed an audience at the City College of New York. The historic land-grant universities had made enormous contributions to American agriculture, he said, "by turning their backs on the then-established model of a college." He called for the creation of sixty-seven urban grant universities, equal to the total number of land-grant universities, "at least one for each city of over a quarter of a million and several for the very large cities." These institutions would "have an aggressive approach to the problems of the city, where the city itself and its problems would become the animating focus."[14]

Kerr acknowledged that the complexity of city problems greatly exceeded those of rural areas, but claimed that "this very complexity makes the prospect of confronting them more important and more challenging." These institutions should provide vastly greater access to higher education for low-income inner-city black students, he maintained, and could work to improve urban school systems through "school agents," counterparts to the land-grant county-agents. Urban grant universities also would address health and environmental problems and could help revitalize depressed urban areas in which they were located. Kerr argued that urban grant universities should be substantially funded by the federal government, and he proposed that unlike the Morrill Act, which left the selection of land-grant institutions to the states, these urban grant universities be selected directly by the federal government from applications by public, private, existing, or new colleges. Some five months later, Kerr delivered a major address in Massachusetts in which elaborated on this plan. Soon thereafter, the US Office of Education printed and distributed it.[15]

Although the US Office of Education did not endorse Kerr's proposal, it commissioned a survey of urban universities, published in 1970. In the foreword to the report of this survey, Preston Valien, deputy associate commissioner for higher education, acknowledged the importance of the Morrill Act to American higher education but explained that colleges and universities "located in a large city, need help of another kind." The cities, he said, are turning to the universities "for help in solving what has come to be known as the 'urban crisis,' but few if any universities find themselves prepared to respond to this request."[16]

In that same year, the Ombudsman Foundation of Los Angeles called for the establishment of an urban grant college, which it described as "a college without walls." It asserted that the historic "break with tradition on the part of the Land Grant College could apply equally well to the establishment of the Urban Grant College." One of its major purposes would be "to make the professors 'practical' and the farmer or urban dweller 'scientific.'"[17]

Two years later, the prestigious Carnegie Commission on Higher Education issued an elaborate report called *The Campus and the City*. It acknowledged the analogy, now widely drawn, between land-grant universities and the needs of cities but asserted that the land-grant model provided "no close parallel" to the needs of cities:

> The universities did make enormous contributions to agricultural productivity and to the quality of rural life. But they were aided by great breakthroughs in the biological sciences, particularly in genetics. No similar breakthroughs have occurred in the area of the study of urban problems. The social sciences, in particular, are not now prepared to make the same contribution to the city as the biological sciences have made to the rural economy. . . . Also, in the case of agriculture, the land-grant universities dealt with a few interest groups; the city involves many. And the land grant institutions were usually new institutions performing new functions; while there will be some new urban universities, the new services to the city will mostly come from older institutions slowly taking on new duties.

Yet despite these reservations, the report called for urban grant allocations by HUD of $10 million annually to ten colleges and universities "to see what they can do with imaginative overall approaches to urban problems."[18]

In 1976, four years after the Carnegie report, leaders of twenty universities located in major cities across the country founded the Committee on Urban Public Universities to lobby for urban grant legislation. They put out a call for a national urban grant universities program, stating that while public universities in cities were "originally established primarily from state and local investments, they are now in a position to provide a national service if complementary federal and private resources are added."[19]

The committee engaged a full-time lobbyist in Washington. One of the group's leaders, President James Olson of the University of Missouri, wrote that "federal support enabled the land-grant colleges to develop their research and service activities without direct reference to enrollments," and the continued development of the research and service activities of the newer urban universities required similar support. The committee soon determined that it could enhance its chances for success in Congress if it included private universities located in large cities in the grant legislation. It, therefore, changed its name to the Committee for Urban Program Universities, significantly altering its vision as well.[20]

In 1978, the Subcommittee on Postsecondary Education of the House Committee on Education and Labor held a series of hearings in five different cities on an Urban Grant University Act, which would authorize up to $25 million a year to aid "urban universities to develop their capacity to help find answers to urban problems" and to "make their educational, research, and service capabilities more readily and effectively available to the urban communities in which they are located." The act defined urban universities as institutions located in urban areas with a substantial part of their enrollment coming from the local area. The legislation required qualifying institutions to develop programs to give local students greater access to postsecondary education, offer a "wide range of professional or graduate programs," and have "demonstrated and sustained a sense of responsibility" to their urban area and its people. Numerous higher education leaders testified at these hearings, often spelling out in detail the current public service programs of their institutions.[21]

The National League of Cities supported the legislation, noting that the urban observatories program "was beneficial for both the universities and the cities that participated" and that it laid a foundation for this program. However, reflecting the tensions that surfaced in the urban observatory program, it urged that the bill be amended to mandate that cities must play a major role in determining what problems would be addressed by the urban grant institutions.[22] Congress enacted the bill and President Jimmy Carter signed it in October 1980. It passed again, with some changes, in 1986. But Congress never appropriated funds for this program.

State University Systems

The "urban crisis" put increasing pressure on state officials to expand the presence of their public universities in major cities. State governments, however, continued to display skepticism about cities in general and urban slums in particular. The rapid growth of the suburbs reinforced this anti-urbanism and diminished the representation of cities in state legislatures. Nonetheless, the democratization of higher education in general, coupled with the growing demand to greatly increase the number of college-educated African Americans meant that state governments would have to respond somehow.

Efforts to address this need aggravated the long-standing tensions between established flagship and land-grant universities and the new urban institutions. At a 1967 conference on higher education and the vitality of cities, Stanford University education professor Lewis Mayhew complained that "Higher Education has not successfully brought its influence to bear to the service of the non-white population" in cities. He argued that municipal universities like Wayne, Cincinnati, Houston, Toledo, and Louisville, which from their inception had played an important role in their cities, had been taken over by their states and now focused on state and national needs and sought national stature. The same dynamic diminished the urban focus of private institutions taken over by state university systems, like the University of Pittsburgh and Temple University.[23]

In the mid-1960s, Richard Lugar, mayor of Indianapolis, demanded that a comprehensive state-funded university be created in his city. Both Indiana University in Bloomington and Purdue University in Lafayette had branch campuses in Indianapolis. The presidents of those two institutions, fearing competition from a new public university in the state's largest city, got their boards and the state legislature to merge their Indianapolis campuses and create IUPUI (Indiana University–Purdue University–Indianapolis). The legislation gave Indiana University's administration "exclusive responsibility" for the new institution, thereby limiting IUPUI's independence.[24]

The opposition of the University of Massachusetts administration in Amherst and the private colleges in Boston to the expansion of the university into the city continued through the 1960s. The state legislature, which created the University of Massachusetts Boston, also legislated establishment of a medical school as part of the state university. Many people thought the new medical school should be located in Boston, but the existing Boston medical schools (Harvard, Tufts, and Boston University) lobbied vigorously against that location, and ultimately the state built it in Worcester.

In 1966, a long-range plan for the three-campus university drafted by a senior administrator in Amherst, called for doctoral programs to be concentrated in Amherst and for the Boston campus to emphasize undergraduate education. In 1970, the university's trustees restructured the institution's governance, with a single president for the system to whom chancellors at each campus reported. The renowned urban scholar, Robert Wood, became the first system president, and he opened the presidential office in Boston, a short distance from the state house.[25]

Tensions also continued at already established urban campuses in state systems. Despite President Fred H. Harrington and Chancellor J. Martin Klotsche's 1963 plan to establish "major university status" for the University of Wisconsin–Milwaukee, the staff of the state's Coordinating Committee for Higher Education (CCHE) prepared a series of reports in 1968 suggesting instead that UWM strive to be "a high quality urban university." The reports questioned whether Wisconsin could afford a second major university. CCHE also delayed approval of Milwaukee PhD programs in chemistry and anthropology for over two years.

Interestingly, in 1966 President Harrington addressed the annual meeting of the AUU. He recognized that urban universities were increasingly pursuing basic and theoretical research and that they sought to increase the "number of high-quality, full-time resident students." But he urged AUU members not to give up "the commuting student, the part-time student," and "applied research, extension and public service." If schools take on the goals of the high prestige universities, he warned, "they will cease to be urban universities as you would normally wish to define them."[26]

Urban Renewal and Neighborhood Relations

By the mid-1960s, as the neighborhoods adjacent to universities became increasingly poor and black, and as expanding enrollment caused them to contemplate land acquisition and expansion, higher education leaders, scholars, and journalists devoted more and more attention to the relationship between universities and their neighbors. For example, in 1964 the *Journal of Higher Education* published an article on the uses of urban renewal for campus expansion.[27] In 1967, *Teachers College Record* presented an essay by a California planning official calling for the integration of expanding urban universities with their surrounding cities.[28] In 1968, *Business Week* described how "colleges learn their urban ABCs," meaning how they responded to backlash from their neighboring "ghetto communities."[29] Fred Hechinger, who wrote on higher education for the *New York Times*, published a column entitled "The Urban University: Relationship of College to Its Neighbors Called the Root of Today's Problems."[30] A year later, *Change* magazine published four articles in one issue under the title

"Confrontation: The Campus and the City." Boston mayor Kevin White authored the lead article.[31] A 1969 journal article on urban higher education described "the crisis in university-urban relations," concluding that the universities must solve this problem: "How can the institution which is located in an ever increasingly black central city expand and serve the people living around it without lowering its standards and destroying homes?"[32] And in 1971, *Minerva* also published an analysis of universities and their response to neighborhood deterioration.[33]

Writers paid special attention to neighborhood tensions at Columbia University and the University of Pennsylvania. Columbia's Morningside Heights neighborhood had a growing number of low-income residents, mostly African American and Puerto Rican. Columbia's provost Jacques Barzun told the city's Board of Estimate in 1965 that the neighborhood had become "uninviting, abnormal, sinister and dangerous" and explained that Columbia needed "a decent residential neighborhood."[34] In the 1950s and early 1960s, Columbia purchased numerous deteriorating buildings adjacent to campus, forcing many of these buildings' residents to leave. Columbia also worked with a city government agency to develop an urban renewal plan for Harlem, between 125th and 135th Streets, in which the university would build faculty and student housing as well as housing for tenants displaced from Morningside Heights.

Huge protests erupted after Columbia began construction of a new gymnasium on 2.1 acres of the city-owned Morningside Park. Mayor Robert Wagner and Parks Commissioner Robert Moses agreed that Columbia could lease the property from the city for a hundred years for the modest sum of $3,000 per year. The gym building would also include a separate facility for the community, with a separate entrance facing Harlem. By 1967, significant opposition to the project emerged from the black community, some of whose activists called it a "racist gym." Some students called it "gym crow." After substantial delay as the university sought to placate community leaders, the Columbia began construction on February 19, 1968. The following day twenty people staged a sit-in adjacent to bulldozers and dump trucks, and police arrested six Columbia students active in civil rights and six community residents. A week later, students and neighborhood residents held a larger demonstration, resulting in additional arrests. On April 8, the Students' Afro-American Society published an open letter in the campus newspaper, complaining about Columbia's failure to relate successfully to black students, warning that "until the university and other institutions change many of their basic policies there will be no end to

Protest against Columbia University gym construction, 1968. Photograph © Lee T. Pearcy.

racial animosity and violence." One of the flyers distributed by student protesters was headlined "The people will run Columbia or the people will burn it down." Other protests followed. Then on April 23, students took over Low Library, protesting both the gym and the university's involvement in weapons research and the war in Vietnam. Within a week, the university halted construction on the gym.[35] Ultimately, the university built a new gym at another location on campus.

The West Philadelphia Corporation, which included community officials on its board along with representatives of the University of Pennsylvania, Drexel, and other educational and cultural institutions, made significant progress in redevelopment of the University City neighborhood in the in the mid-1960s and the 1970s. It developed an urban renewal plan for approximately 200 acres of land to the north and west of Penn and Drexel. The city transferred a small portion of the land to the two universities for construction of new facilities. The urban renewal plan designated a much larger portion of the area for demolition of deteriorated buildings, acquisition of vacant land, and construction of housing and facilities for the Pennsylvania Medical School, the University City Science Center, and several other structures. In 1967, the city received

Student protest flyer, Columbia University, 1968.

$12 million in federal urban renewal money for this purpose. The plan faced significant opposition from people living in the area. The NAACP, Congress on Racial Equality, and the Student Non-violent Coordinating Committee organized a variety of protests.[36]

The University of Pennsylvania's role in urban renewal stemmed in large part from its goal of transforming itself into an elite residential research university. Well before the initiation of the University City urban renewal project, Penn began extensive student housing construction. In 1966, fewer than 30 percent of all full-time students lived on campus. By 1972, more than 50 percent did so. Part-time enrollment dropped from 7,360 in 1965 to 4,489 in

1972.[37] Urban renewal's impact on the racial and socioeconomic composition of the campus neighborhood played a key role in the university's transformation to a national institution.

In 1965, the State of Pennsylvania took over Temple University. This substantially increased enrollment, and Temple accelerated its property acquisition and construction. In 1966, local residents organized protests against the university's expansion. Temple's growth since the 1950s had displaced about seven thousand residents. In response, the university declared a moratorium on construction in the residential area west of Broad Street.

A new president, Paul Anderson, assumed office in 1967 and began a range of efforts to mitigate conflict with neighborhood residents. In 1969, the university started a series of planning "charrettes" with community representatives and city, state, and federal officials to develop a campus neighborhood plan that all could accept. No agreement emerged, however, so state officials mediated negotiations leading to the Community-Temple Agreement of 1970. Temple reduced its institutional development district by thirteen acres and agreed to building height limits on some of its properties. Temple also committed itself to seek community approval of future development plans. In addition, the university modified its admissions standards for minority students and provided them with tutorial and financial assistance, significantly increasing enrollment from North Philadelphia.[38]

North of Harlem, Columbia University Medical School faced its own troubles. Faculty and students saw Washington Heights as a dangerous neighborhood, and medical school officials believed this location hindered faculty recruitment. The medical school administration contemplated leaving the city, but in 1982 a long-range planning committee concluded that it should remain in Washington Heights. The school acquired six acres of land east of Broadway that had no residential buildings, eliminating the problem of resident displacement that had been so problematic in Morningside Heights. Tension did develop over Columbia's acquisition of the shuttered Audubon Ballroom, where Malcolm X had been assassinated. This caused some black militants to oppose Columbia's acquisition of the property, but the university reached agreement in 1992 with the city, elected officials, community, and Black Muslim leaders.[39]

Much of the Bronx underwent a similar decline, as middle-class whites moved to the suburbs and poor African Americans and Puerto Ricans moved there in large numbers. New York University's Heights campus had opened in 1894 to provide a countrified residential environment for full-time students.

But by the late 1960s, NYU administrators were concerned about the campus's future. University Heights sat to the west of the Grand Concourse, a street running through the Bronx with attractive middle-class housing. In the mid-1960s, various newspaper articles suggested that the Grand Concourse and the west Bronx might soon face dramatic decline even though at the time this area remained largely middle-class. As fears about the future of the west Bronx increased, enrollments at NYU Heights declined 15 percent in 1969, 20 percent in 1970, and 40 percent in 1971. The next year, NYU sold its Heights campus to City University of New York for $62 million. The campus then became home to Bronx Community College.[40]

At Fordham University's Rose Hill campus, continued neighborhood deterioration threatened this historic Bronx institution. Anxiety grew following several crimes, much publicized, against students and faculty. Raymond Schroth, a Jesuit priest who spent his career at Fordham's Bronx campus, wrote in a memoir that "in the 1970s, on and off campus, we watched 'our city' crumble before our eyes."[41] Fordham had already shifted some programs to its new facilities at Lincoln Center in Manhattan. But it also sought to improve the neighborhood adjacent to the Rose Hill campus. In 1968, it established an administrative position of "neighborhood liaison" assigned to engage Fordham with the Morris Heights Neighborhood Improvement Association and the Community Planning Board. Fordham also created the Northwest Bronx Community and Clergy Coalition. The group developed a plan for Fordham Plaza, which would house an office building, a department store, a parking garage, and shops on two blocks across the street from the campus. The US Postal Service owned the land on which the plaza would be built, and for ten years resisted demands that it sell it. In October 1974, two months after NYU sold its Bronx campus, Fordham's president threatened to relocate to property the university owned in suburban Westchester County. New York's Urban Development Corporation then took over responsibility for the Fordham Plaza project, and in 1982 it succeeded in getting the postal service to transfer the land. A developer broke ground for the plaza shortly thereafter.[42]

In the 1970s, Saint Louis University also undertook projects to upgrade the neighborhoods surrounding its two campuses in midtown St. Louis. President Paul Reinert later explained that "the university found itself engulfed in the midst of an urban crisis that endangered its continued vitality." He said that the crisis stemmed from decay, population loss, abandoned buildings, crime, and an increasingly transient population. The university worked with neighborhood residents, businessmen, and institutional representatives to create New Town/St. Louis Inc., a nonprofit organization that oversaw extensive redevelopment, in 1974. Reinert, undoubtedly well aware of university-neighborhood tensions in many cities, argued that "instead of trying to impose its own redevelopment scheme upon the community, the university helped mobilize neighborhood residents" to address the decline of these areas.[43]

Wayne State University, at the request of Detroit's director of city planning, established a joint planning committee with the city to develop University City on 302 acres bordering the campus; the area was to be used for university expansion and neighborhood development. Community opposition proved very strong, however. In 1965, a coalition of churches, block clubs, and school groups founded the West Central Organization, led by activist clergy, to oppose University City. They argued that the area was not a "slum" but simply a neighborhood most of whose residents were African American. Critics also complained that the plan made no provision to move displaced residents to comparable housing elsewhere in the city. Wayne State moved forward despite the opposition, building a Physical Education and Recreation Building, which opened in 1967, and a football stadium completed the following year.

Local residents vigorously opposed the next phase of University City development and twice got the Detroit Common Council to reduce its size. The *Detroit Free Press* ran a series of articles highly critical of University City, and Coleman Young, a state senator, held legislative hearings about this urban renewal project. Wayne scaled back its plans for the second phase in 1971 and by the middle of the decade abandoned it completely.[44]

Conflict over construction plans was not restricted to low-income neighborhoods. Loyola University in Baltimore, a commuter institution serving local students, decided in the 1960s to build national stature by attracting strong students from outside of Baltimore and Maryland. It developed plans in 1966 to construct three dormitories over five years, to accommodate four hundred students, nearly half of the enrollment of full-time undergraduates. The university built these residence halls on the edge of campus, overlooking the back yards of four large private houses. Although the homeowners had no way to stop construction, they and others in the neighborhood developed deep suspicions about the university's plans for the future.

In 1975, the university moved administrative offices to a building previously used as the president's home, and residents filed complaints with the zoning board and in court. Toward the end of the decade, the neighborhood association challenged Loyola's request for a zoning variance to build bleachers on its athletic field and light poles around the field. Public hearings followed, but the university prevailed.[45]

Shortly after the passage of section 112, in 1959, Nashville mayor Ben West encouraged Vanderbilt University to develop an urban renewal plan, which the city council authorized in 1961 for a hundred-acre neighborhood adjacent to campus. However, many local residents disputed the premise that the area qualified for federal slum clearance funds. In 1962, the federal government deferred approval of this project until the university could prove that the area was sufficiently poor and deteriorated to qualify for urban renewal status. An article in the *Vanderbilt Law Review* later argued that the land the university sought to acquire "lay in the heart of an exclusively white, predominantly middle-class neighborhood which bore little resemblance to the conventional image of a slum."[46]

The university engaged a consulting firm to study the neighborhood again, and it concluded that it did meet federal criteria for urban renewal. The city in 1967 approved Vanderbilt's urban renewal plan, the University Center Redevelopment Project. Two resident organizations, the University Neighborhood Association and the Committee for the Protection of Private Property undertook various efforts to block Vanderbilt in the courts and the city council. They succeeded in 1973 in getting the city council to remove from the urban renewal area the sixty-eight lots not yet owned by Vanderbilt. Four months later, however, university lobbyists persuaded the council to rescind this action. Various lawsuits proved unsuccessful, and in 1975 the US Supreme Court declined to consider the case. In the end, Vanderbilt used the land acquired for parking, athletic fields, and expansion of its medical center.[47]

Even the University of Wisconsin–Milwaukee, whose chancellor championed the key role of urban universities in the city's development, faced local resistance to campus expansion. In 1969, a member of the Milwaukee City Council introduced a resolution stating that in light of the significant loss of city tax revenue from property owned by the state university, the council "expresses its opposition to any further expansion of the University of Wisconsin–Milwaukee without provision being made to compensate for services rendered by the City to the University and the furnishing of relocation services and payments for the families displaced."[48]

Conflict also occurred over the construction of new universities. The State of New Jersey initiated plans for a new medical university complex in the early 1960s. Initially, officials planned to build it in Madison, an overwhelmingly white suburb twenty-five miles west of Newark. Newark's mayor, however, insisted that it be built in the city and developed a plan to place the complex in a large area of the central ward occupied by low-income black residents, clearing the area through urban renewal. Black opposition emerged quickly, but the mayor continued to move ahead with his plan until Newark's major civil disturbance in 1967, which received massive national attention. New Jersey governor Richard Hughes, under substantial pressure from federal officials in the Departments of Housing and Urban Development and Health, Education, and Welfare, decided in 1968 to establish a formal process for negotiation between city and medical university officials and community leaders. They ultimately reached agreement greatly reducing the amount of land for the medical school, allocating a significant portion of land in the area for housing construction by nonprofit groups, establishing special procedures to ensure that minority contractors received a fair share of the work involved in building the medical complex, and obtaining a guarantee that the medical school and hospital would develop an ongoing program to address the health needs of low-income residents.[49]

In retrospect, many analysts assert that urban renewal coupled with massive low-income housing construction accelerated the deterioration of central cities. It displaced large numbers of low-income minorities, and the massive construction of low-income public housing in particular neighborhoods created new ghettoes and increased racial segregation.[50] Universities played a significant role in urban renewal. Critics claimed that they consciously sought to displace poor residents, to surround their institutions with middle-class residents, and to use urban renewal as a means of acquiring land for expansion. Defenders maintained that universities helped to attract middle-class residents and enriched the city's culture. They also argued that urban renewal enabled universities to acquire badly needed land for expansion, making these institutions even more valuable to the city.

The "urban crisis" dramatically expanded the relationship between city, state, and federal government and universities. Cities, often with state financial support, worked closely with universities on neighborhood urban renewal. State governments also had to fund the expansion of universities in cities and mediate their relationships with the established flagship institutions.

As the federal government sought to address the problems of urban poverty, racism, and the challenges facing city governments, it called on universities and individual scholars to address these needs, and it provided substantial funding through the programs of the Higher Education Act of 1965 and many other initiatives, including the urban observatories. This broadened the role of universities in shaping American cities.

At the same time, by building partnerships with the federal government, as well as with state and local governments, urban higher educational institutions further strengthened the view that community service constituted a central mission for all of American higher education. Although Congress never allocated funds for urban grant universities, advocates, in making the case for them, reinforced the idea that service was integral to the mission of urban universities.

The "urban crisis" had a profound effect on universities in cities, which in turn shaped American higher education overall. City institutions now led the nation's efforts to democratize higher education. They also greatly expanded the meaning of community service and advanced the application of social science research to public policy. Universities had perhaps a modest impact on the future of their cities, but they continued to significantly reshape and expand the mission of American higher education.

6

The Legacy of the Urban Crisis and the Ever-Changing City, 1981–2016

Concern in the 1960s and 1970s about the effects of poverty on low-income and "ghetto" residents in many cities and the physical deterioration of their neighborhoods continued well into the twenty-first century. In many ways, however, cities in the late twentieth century and the early twenty-first century became increasingly attractive to large numbers of Americans. Universities in cities played a role in this change, and they benefited enormously from it.

Manufacturing jobs in cities continued to decline dramatically. In 1982, New York still had 529,000 factory jobs. By 2002, the number had fallen to 143,200. In Chicago the number of factory jobs declined from 277,000 to 97,600; in Los Angeles, from 327,600 to 162,200; and in Detroit, from 105,700 to 38,000.[1] However, employment in research, information and health sciences, finance, marketing, corporate management, and education grew substantially in many cities. Suburbanization continued unabated, and the 2000 census reported that a majority of Americans now lived in suburbs. By 2005, more poor people lived in suburbs than in cities.

Most cities no longer faced declining population, and some cities' populations actually grew. A demographic analysis of the fifty largest metropolitan areas in the United States reported that the per capita income of residents who lived at the center of their city, adjusted for inflation, went from $31,358 in 1990 to $43,394 in 2012. The percentage of these residents with a baccalaureate degree or higher went from 29 percent in 1990 to 49 percent in 2012. Those living in households below the poverty line declined from 31 percent to 22 percent. And the number of adults between the ages of twenty-two and thirty-four also increased dramatically.[2]

These demographic changes reflected the transformation of the economies of many central cities, which increasingly housed rapidly expanding industries like high technology, financial services, business management, and other knowledge-intensive enterprises. At the start of the twenty-first century, central cities and their immediate surroundings housed 1,900 higher education institutions, more than half of the nation's colleges and universities. These institutions spent $136 billion on salaries, goods, and services, and employed two million workers, two-thirds of them in administrative and maintenance positions open to low-skill workers. A 2003 study reported that licenses for products developed in universities and marketed by businesses they incubated had created 270,000 jobs.[3]

In 1994, Harvard Business School professor Michael E. Porter founded Initiative for a Competitive Inner City to "spark new thinking about the business potential of inner cities, thereby creating jobs and wealth for inner-city residents." In 2001, the initiative joined with CEOs for Cities, an organization of business leaders, to prepare a study of the role of colleges and universities in urban economic revitalization. The report argued that in addition to the longstanding role of providing education, health, and social services, higher education institutions "are equally well positioned to spur economic revitalization of our inner cities."[4]

The following year, Richard Florida, a professor of regional economic development at Carnegie Mellon University, published a book arguing that economic development depended on a "creative class," which tended to cluster in some cities, and that universities were "a key institution of the Creative Economy." His analysis received a good deal of attention. A decade later, he asserted in the preface to the new edition his book that initially many people had derided his idea that "the talented were beginning to favor cities over suburbs, that urban centers were challenging suburban industrial park nerdistans [*sic*] as locations for talent and high-tech industry, and that older cities were starting to regain some of the ground they'd lost to Sun Belt boomtowns." Now, he declared, these statements "aren't even controversial."[5] After Barack Obama's election as president in 2008, his incoming secretary of housing and urban development, Shaun Donovan, engaged the Institute for Urban Research at the University of Pennsylvania to develop strategic initiatives for the national economic crisis. The report recommended "building diverse core neighborhoods around anchor institutions and anchor amenities" and stated that cities had "to understand how economic growth can be built on these foundational assets." After publication of its report, the Penn Institute for Urban Research created a national Anchor Institutions Task Force.[6]

In 2012, Campus Compact, a national organization founded in 1985 to encourage college student community service, issued a report calling on universities to go beyond promoting student civic responsibility to create "engaged learning economies." It urged them to develop strong community partnerships and to use them to build the local economy. "Campuses can learn from these partnerships," the report's authors explained, "about how economic engagement can grow businesses, increase employment, open the job market, and use research to inspire economic innovation."[7]

Given these positive developments, it is not surprising that many higher educators asserted a much more positive assessment of universities in cities, arguing that these institutions stood on the cutting edge of the nation's needs and should be different from traditional colleges. This new view of the relationship of universities and cities emerged initially in the ongoing discussion over the definition and mission of the urban university. In 1980, University of Wisconsin–Milwaukee professor Ernest Spaights published an article arguing that many institutions in cities were reluctant to embrace their urban identity because they "equate the term *urban university* with academic inferiority." He described the urban university as a "specialized institution" that should "fulfill its obligation to the city in which it lives" and build "an academic zeal for urbanness."[8] A few months later, the president of the University of Alabama at Birmingham characterized the urban university as a unique type of institution, with a mission of "educating new types of students in a new type of environment," enriching the quality of life in cities, and "assisting in creating a new image for our country's urban areas."[9] In the same year, Wayne State University president Thomas Bonner wrote in the *Chronicle of Higher Education* that the city "provides the raison d'être of the urban university."[10]

Ronald Williams, president of Northern Illinois University in Chicago addressed a conference at the University of Arkansas at Little Rock, "The Urban University: Present and Future," in 1981. He pointed to numerous efforts under way to "transform our cities into vibrant and productive centers" and observed that urban state universities demonstrated "an equal commitment and involvement in rejuvenating our cities." He placed greatest emphasis on the "formidable challenge" of teaching students from very diverse backgrounds.[11] Arnold Grobman published a book on urban state universities in 1988, shortly after completing his eleven-year chancellorship of the University of Missouri–St. Louis.

He, too, argued that an urban university must be "a participating citizen," that the overwhelming majority of students must live in the city or its suburbs, and that it must demonstrate concern for "the massive problems that became exacerbated in the 1960s and remain with us today."[12]

Sheldon Hackney, shortly after stepping down as president of the University of Pennsylvania in 1993, proposed that the nation needed to reinvent its university system because "the problem of the city is the strategic problem of our time." Therefore, properly addressing this problem would significantly contribute to "the university's primary mission of advancing and transmitting knowledge." To do so would create "a morally inspired, real-world focused, problem-solving, urban university system for the twenty-first century."[13] The dean of nursing at the University of Louisville asserted that the urban university "is positioned to recreate the American university" by fostering diversity, educating low-income students, and researching cities and applying that knowledge to the needs of the community.[14]

Two scholars of higher education at Temple University attacked the traditional notion of the collegiate ideal in a pastoral environment, arguing in 1999 that "the urban environment provides an unparalleled opportunity for an intellectual community to test its ideas against the complex reality of life as it is lived in this country's major cities." They also criticized their own institution for moving away from its urban mission and seeking higher prestige through more selective admissions.[15]

A dean at Indiana University–Purdue University–Indianapolis, addressing the Indianapolis Association in 2000, complained that public research universities had become "in-turned, self-indulgent, and arrogant, with many rights and privileges but with responsibility only to themselves." He called for a new kind of university deeply committed to teaching all kinds of students and conducting first-rate applied as well as basic research. A prototype of the ideal twenty-first-century university already existed, he explained, in the urban university. He acknowledged, however, that "it has gone largely unrecognized" because these institutions "are often underfunded, don't have football teams, and their function is viewed as one of rendering only local service to working students who can't go anywhere else and who need little intellectual stimulation." This distorted view did not recognize the importance of teaching a broad cross-section of students, of being of "immediate and direct relevance to social issues," and of undertaking basic and applied research equally well.[16]

A few academicians dissented from this seeming consensus. Harold Enarson, who had served as president of Ohio State University, argued against Bonner's position in the same issue of the *Chronicle*. He stated that "the dream of a distinctly urban" institution of higher education was "more remote than ever." He insisted that it was "an idea whose time, fortunately, has passed."[17]

Most who disagreed with the bold vision of the urban university as a radically new institution intimately tied to its surroundings believed that there were limits on what higher educational institutions could and should do. David Adamany, who succeeded Bonner as president of Wayne, strongly supported engagement with the city, but he drew clear parameters around the kinds of service universities could provide. He contended that universities should expand their research on cities and "more fully explore the applications of knowledge" to the problems confronting their communities. He also insisted that universities provide access to low-income students from disadvantaged backgrounds and to adults on and off campus, work with their cities' public school systems to better prepare students for college, keep tuition low, and conduct scholarship on urban needs. But he warned against universities providing public services not connected to teaching and research. Universities lacked the ability "to operate large-scale urban economic or social programs." Good citizenship for them, he argued, "means fulfilling—with excellence—their principal missions of teaching and scholarship within the context of urban life."[18] Interestingly, Adamany faced significant faculty opposition implementing his version of this circumscribed definition of Wayne's urban mission.

Interest in cities and urban universities continued to engage many higher education organizations despite the idea that urban universities had low status. Although the Association of Urban Universities shut down in 1977 due to declining interest in its activities on the part of university presidents, several national university associations fostered significant discussion of cities and their problems. In 1982, the National Association of State Universities and Land-Grant Colleges (NASULGC) in cooperation with the National Research Council's Committee on National Urban Policy held a three-day invitational meeting of urban university presidents and chancellors. One of the conference organizers explained to those attending that "there have been no clear-cut models for the urban university" as there have been for research and land-grant universities; therefore, he hoped that the discussion would lead to "alternative models . . . and new ways for the urban university to plan for future urban change."[19]

The following year, NASULGC published a study on the status of cities and their universities, with recommendations for both the institutions and for local and national policy makers. It called for improved relationships between universities and their local environments, attention to the best ways to evaluate faculty at urban institutions in light of the demands of teaching underprepared students and of conducting applied urban research, improving relationships with government, addressing the problems of the city through research, and developing ways of meeting the needs of students "inadequately prepared in the local school systems."[20] NASULGC's Urban Affairs Division shortly thereafter published a detailed report on university-city interactions, listing numerous centers and programs that worked with their respective cities, such as at Wayne State, University of Wisconsin–Milwaukee, University of Tennessee at Chattanooga, University of Missouri–St. Louis, University of Illinois at Chicago, University of Cincinnati, University of Delaware, Kent State, and Rutgers.

Community Engagement by Students

In 1989, leaders of several urban institutions established a new organization, the Coalition of Urban and Metropolitan Universities. Three of its founders detailed the organization's mission in the first issue of its journal, *Metropolitan Universities*. It had striking similarities to the vision of an urban university a few decades earlier. "The university must not stand apart from its society and its immediate environment," they wrote, "but must be an integral part of that society. The university best serves itself and society by assuming an active leadership role, as opposed to its traditional stance of somewhat passive responsiveness." A metropolitan university "must extend its resources to the surrounding region, to work cooperatively with the region's schools, municipalities, businesses, industries, and the many other institutions and organizations in the public and private sectors." They also acknowledged that a metropolitan university could not do everything asked of it. And they stated that these institutions enrolled mostly local commuters and significant numbers of students "not well prepared to succeed in university studies."[21]

Despite this mission statement, some argued that the term "metropolitan" represented a way of avoiding the negative connotation of "urban."[22] By including suburban universities, CUMU had a much broader potential membership and attracted a significant number of institutions outside of central cities interested in connecting to their suburban communities or with their central cities. Unlike the AUU, CUMU focused on community engagement of faculty and students in any geographic location, not just on the social problems of central cities. Indeed, the founders stated that "a metropolitan university is defined first and foremost" by its commitment to "its relationship to the surrounding metropolitan region as its essential rationale," not solely by its location, its student population, or any other characteristic. Acknowledging implicitly CUMU's predecessor, the AUU, they noted that the term "urban" "refers in the minds of many of our constituents only to the core or central city." The metropolitan university "must address the challenges of the inner city as one facet of its overall responsibility." And these challenges, they pointed out quite accurately, could not be remedied without attention to the entire metropolitan area.[23]

In a similar vein, NASULGC, the organization representing land-grant universities, issued a report in 2001 summarizing studies by the Kellogg Foundation on the future of state universities. Entitled *Returning to Our Roots*, it acknowledged many people's frustration at public universities' unresponsiveness to community problems, "despite the resources and expertise available on our campuses." The report's authors insisted that land-grant universities must become "engaged institutions," and they needed "a new emphasis on urban revitalization" comparable to their "rural development efforts in the last century."[24]

Universities in cities had long used experiential learning in their communities to enhance teaching, and they no longer felt the need to explain or justify it. In 1971, a group of educators, businesspeople, and civic leaders created the National Society for Experiential Education (NSEE) to improve experiential education nationwide. It launched its Distinguished Fellows awards in 2014 to honor "key scholars in this field." In 1974, what is now the Council for Adult and Experiential Learning (CAEL) began efforts to assess what students learned from activities and experiences beyond the classroom. Universities across the country increasingly embraced "experiential learning," and it became widespread across American higher education. CAEL continues to this day. Other higher education organizations have also embraced its goal. In 1995, for example, the Association for the Study of Higher Education and George Washington University published an analysis of the research literature on experiential learning, noting "renewed academic interest" in this subject.[25]

One form of experiential education, called "service learning," received particular attention.[26] Urban higher education institutions had long encouraged volunteer community service by students. Given higher education's history of anti-urban bias, urban university leaders expressed deep commitment to building civic responsibility in their students, especially the large number who came from working-class immigrant and African American communities. Since the 1980s, universities, and not just those in cities, have greatly increased efforts to promote volunteer service by students in their local communities.

In 1985, the presidents of Brown, Georgetown, and Stanford Universities, along with the president of the Education Commission of the States, founded Campus Compact to encourage universities to facilitate community engagement and thereby promote responsible citizenship on the part of college graduates. Eleven hundred colleges and universities belonged to Campus Compact in 2016, and its website indicated that 1.8 million students engaged in community service in these institutions. In 2011, it began awarding Civic Fellowships to college students "who have demonstrated an investment in finding solutions for challenges facing communities throughout the country," describing them as "the next generation of public problem solvers and civic leaders."[27]

Higher education scholars wrote extensively about the value of service learning and the best ways to implement it. The American Association for Higher Education published many books on the subject in the late 1990s, including several volumes devoted to service learning in accounting, psychology, biology, peace studies, sociology, communications, religious studies, Spanish, engineering, political science and other disciplines. The Association for the Study of Higher Education also released several books on this subject, as did other scholarly presses.[28] The *Journal of Higher Education* ran a number of articles on service learning as well. An issue once peripheral to American higher education now became central as a result of the activities of urban and metropolitan universities.

Efforts to promote service learning emerged not only from the idea that it would enhance student learning but also from a growing national concern that many young Americans lacked a sense of civic responsibility. In 2000, the American Council on Education distributed a collection of twenty-one essays entitled *Civic Responsibility and Higher Education*. Its editor, Thomas Ehrlich, former president of Indiana University, and his co-author explained in the preface that the earliest American colleges had two equally important purposes, development of student character and of intellect. They acknowledged that contemporary higher education was quite different because "the student bodies served are far more diverse than at any time in our history, in terms of age, race, gender and socioeconomic status." This diversity could be used to support moral and civic learning, but they expressed great concern that it could "make the development of a cohesive campus community," the optimal environment for learning, more difficult.[29]

Barbara Jacoby, a University of Maryland scholar of higher education whose published books included a study of service learning, edited *Civic Engagement in Higher Education*, published in 2009. In her historical introduction, she stated that in the 1980s "Americans were alarmed by growing concern over apathy of citizens in general and of college students in particular." She reviewed several federal government initiatives to address this problem in general but also specifically in higher education, including the National and Community Service Trust Act of 1993. She catalogued a host of organizations supporting civic engagement of college students, including Campus Compact, the Association of American Colleges and Universities, and the American Democracy Project of the Association of State Colleges and Universities. The Democracy Project worked with colleges across the country to encourage student political engagement, jury duty service, and stewardship of public lands, among other areas of service.[30]

Given the emergence of this broad interest in community engagement within higher education, the Carnegie Fund for the Advancement of Teaching added a new category to its system of classifying higher education institutions. The system, begun in 1970, categorized each institution by the level of its programs (e.g., PhD-granting, four-year undergraduate, two-year community college, etc.) and by characteristics of each degree program. In 2006, Carnegie added a voluntary "community engagement" classification to describe "the collaboration between institutions of higher education and their larger communities (local, regional/state, national, global) for the mutually beneficial exchange of knowledge and resources in a context of partnership and reciprocity." By 2015, Carnegie had classified 361 institutions as community engaged.[31]

Federal agencies strongly supported the movement to increase civic engagement among college students. In 1990, President Bush signed legislation creating a Commission on National and Community Service to support service-learning programs. President Clinton expanded the program in 1994 and renamed it the Corporation for National and Community Service, sponsoring a variety of service programs including AmeriCorps.[32] In 2012, the Obama administration Department of Education released a report urging colleges and universities to make civic learning and democratic engagement "an animating national priority." In the wake of this report, numerous institutions launched civic learning and engagement initiatives. *Inside Higher Education* ran a major story in 2016 entitled "Colleges Placing Increasing Importance on Programs Promoting Civic Engagement."[33] Community engagement, begun decades earlier by institutions in cities, now pervaded American higher education.

Urban Research and Engaged Scholarship

Scholars of urban affairs in large cities now devoted significant attention to the problems of their own municipalities. In 1978, as New York City struggled with its severe financial crisis, the Conservation of Human Resources Project at Columbia University and the Center for New York City Affairs at the New School established the Setting Municipal Priorities Project, aimed at building "a sustained capability within New York City for high quality analytic research" on budget and policy options. Co-directed by a professor of public administration and a professor of business, the project sought to provide an independent source of data and analysis to address the city's fiscal problems. The reports issued, however, faced controversy. Shortly after the release of each report, the directors held a conference to discuss its implications. In 1981, Mayor Edward Koch refused to attend because he viewed the previous year's report as critical of him, and he prohibited other city officials from participating. That report had said that while city government policies had succeeded in balancing the budget, "the greatest burden was borne by the city's poor, whose standard of living was reduced." The head of the city's largest public employee union supported Koch. Still, the three candidates for governor of New York State all spoke at the conference opening.[34]

In the same year as this controversy, New York University established a cross-disciplinary Urban Research Center to conduct policy-oriented research on the problems of New York City and its metropolitan area. Its initial research agenda consisted of studies of the city's economy, crime and the criminal justice system, social services, and housing. A brochure describing the center explained that it sought interaction with the New York business community and with public policy makers "so that the Center's researchers are aware of how policy problems are seen in the business community," as well as to ensure that the business community was aware of the policy solutions put forward by the center.[35]

Later in the decade, University of Chicago sociologist William Julius Wilson secured external funding for the Urban Family Life and Poverty Project to study the relationship of family structure to poverty in Chicago. He continued work on this issue for many years, resulting in numerous publications with broad implications for public policy. His book *The Truly Disadvantaged: The Inner City, the Underclass, and Public Policy* won numerous awards and received significant public attention.[36] In the early 1990s, the Foundation for Child Development established a Neighborhoods Research Grants Program, providing scholars at several institutions with research funds to develop ways to evaluate initiatives seeking to improve neighborhood and family conditions in the researcher's city.[37]

Scholars also continued to assess the impact of urban research on policy and the conditions of cities. In 1988, Nathan Glazer observed that the expectation that urban research at universities could deal with the problems of cities "has not been fulfilled." Advocates of this kind of problem-oriented research had engaged in "unwarranted optimism about what could be known about the causes and solutions" of the urban crisis in general and New York City in particular. He went on to suggest that universities could help to ameliorate the urban crisis only by continuing to do "that for which they are best qualified: education and research."[38]

Ira Harkavy, a historian at the University of Pennsylvania, took the opposite view. The plagues of "crack, crime, AIDS and homelessness" manifesting severe problems in the social system encouraged a change in the "dominant culture" of universities, he wrote, causing them to show concern over such matters, which they had ignored previously.[39] Two years later, David Adamany argued that universities' traditional research mission aligned perfectly with "the service role of universities in urban settings." Elite research universities, although enrolling relatively few local residents, now needed to play a major role in urban life through research.[40] At a 1998 global conference in Amsterdam on universities and cities, NYU historian Tom Bender complained that "it is astonishing how few social scientists (outside of professional schools) at . . . NYU and Columbia, are studying the [urban] issues on everyone's mind."[41]

Nonetheless, the growing movement for civic engagement of college students and university academic programs created significant enthusiasm for "engaged scholarship." In 1999, Pennsylvania State University, Ohio State University, and the University of Wisconsin extension program organized an "outreach scholarship" conference that brought together academicians interested in connecting their research to the needs of their communities. Following the conference, its organizers created a coordinating organization called the Outreach Scholarship Partnership. In 2013 the organization changed its name to the Engagement Scholarship Consortium. Its stated purposes included "encouraging the realization that the scholarship of engagement is a critical aspect of university responsibility" and conducting and disseminating research on "the impact of campus-community partnerships." In 2016, its website listed nearly fifty journals devoted to community-engaged scholarship, university outreach, and service learning. These included the *Engaged Scholar Journal*, *International Journal of Civic Engagement and Social Change*, *Journal for Civic Commitment*, *Journal of Community Engagement and Higher Education*, *Journal of Public Scholarship in Higher Education*, *Journal of Service-Learning in Higher Education*, and *Undergraduate Journal of Service-Learning and Community-Based Research*.[42] Clearly, pursuit of engaged scholarship was becoming more mainstream in American higher education.

In 1996, the University of Massachusetts Boston created an award for faculty professional service and academic outreach, named for Ernest Lynton, a pioneer advocate of university service to its community. In 2007, it changed the award name to the Ernest Lynton Award for the Scholarship of Engagement. The website of the New England Resource Center for Higher Education, the entity that sponsored the initial Lynton award, explains that this change "represents a shift from a more unilateral, expert-driven approach to outreach that prevailed in the 80s and early 90s" and often got in the way of constructive university-community collaboration. Instead, it calls for scholars "to go beyond 'service,' with its overtones of noblesse oblige" to "genuine collaboration."[43] In 2006, the Engagement Scholarship Conference joined with the Association of Public and Land-Grant Universities (APLU, formerly the National Association of State Universities and Land Grant Colleges [NASULGC]) and the W. K. Kellogg Foundation to establish four annual Community Engagement Scholarship Awards and one C. Peter Magrath Award, presented at the APLU annual conference.[44] The idea of scholarship connected to the university's surrounding community, long articulated by urban university advocates, now infused higher education well beyond cities.

Neighborhood Relations

Tensions and collaborations between universities and their neighborhoods continued well into the twenty-first century. Universities in cities faced the long-standing problems of neighborhood deterioration and poverty. However, university presidents and planners, knowing more and more about the history of university involvement in neighborhood urban renewal, actively sought to collaborate with neighborhood residents to avoid triggering community opposition and protest.

Having decided to remain in the Bronx, Fordham University joined with the Northwest Bronx Community and Clergy Coalition to form the University Neighborhood Housing Program. It worked to create and maintain affordable housing in low- and moderate-income neighborhoods in the northwest Bronx, providing low-interest loans for construction projects and predevelopment costs and technical assistance to nonprofit developers. Fordham also opened a twenty-story residence hall on its Lincoln Center campus in 1993, with rooms for 850 students.[45]

Marquette University faced deep concerns about campus safety. Between 1986 and 1991, six Marquette students were murdered off campus. In 1991, it became known that the serial killer Jeffrey Dahmer had lived close to campus and that police found the remains of eleven young men in his apartment. Marquette purchased the building and tore it down. It then spent $50 million to buy 115 other neighborhood properties in the next two years, which it demolished or renovated. Marquette's president, Albert DiUlio, also initiated a program to bring students, faculty, and staff together with neighborhood residents to coordinate neighborhood anti-crime efforts. An editorial in the *Milwaukee Journal* praised DiUlio's response, describing it as a major change in the university's traditional aloofness toward its neighborhood, noting that three years earlier Marquette had displayed "callousness . . . toward permanent residents of the downtown YMCA when MU took over the facility for student housing." By 1999, crime in the neighborhood had fallen by 50 percent and enrollment had increased substantially. Marquette also lobbied the city council, unsuccessfully, to reroute the main street leading to downtown so that it would not run through campus. Community activists criticized Marquette sharply for this, charging that it sought to isolate itself from the city.[46]

The University of Pennsylvania continued to face problems from the surrounding neighborhood and worked to address these. Street crime remained a serious threat. In 1980, black teenagers murdered a student in West Philadelphia. Seventy-one armed robberies and 328 burglaries occurred on campus that year. President Sheldon Hackney responded in a variety of ways. He established the Center for Community Partnerships (now the Netter Center) to support the community through service learning and student volunteer work, to work closely with public schools, and to undertake research of importance to the neighborhood. The West Philadelphia Corporation continued its neighborhood redevelopment projects. However, to avoid further tensions with working-class black neighbors, the university increased the role of community leaders in the corporation and its redevelopment decisions, changing its name to the West Philadelphia Partnership. The City Science Center, initially criticized by some local activists who saw it as part of the university's continuing expansion, proved quite successful in helping to rebuild Philadelphia's declining economy. By 1986, it housed eighty companies and organizations and employed over six thousand people, although few of them came from West Philadelphia. By 1988 it housed twelve buildings. But although it expressed commitment to "combat community deterioration," it did so only on its own land. The university also purchased several deteriorated apartment buildings and renovated them for moderate-income families at affordable rates. Penn also attracted private developers to build housing and retail on university-owned property.

Yet shortly after Judith Rodin assumed the Penn presidency in 1994, five African American youths robbed and murdered a PhD candidate in mathematics at a phone booth eight blocks west of campus. The crime rate in West Philadelphia remained very high. Rodin responded by greatly expanding campus police and security efforts. She also invested millions of dollars in West Philadelphia initiatives and leveraged millions more in private investments. She worked vigorously to build University City as a center of education, retail, and cultural life.[47]

Similar issues emerged in smaller cities. Ohio State University leaders articulated concern about significant neighborhood decline in Columbus. The murder of an undergraduate student in Weinland Park, an area adjacent to the campus, dramatically increased campus anxieties. By the 1990s low-income African Americans constituted a majority of the neighborhood's residents. President Gordon Gee established the nonprofit Campus Partners for Community Urban Redevelopment in 1995 and provided it with annual funding. Ohio State also provided cash incentives to encourage university employees to purchase houses in any of the neighborhoods adjacent to campus. Campus Partners undertook a community-based planning process to formulate a comprehensive University Neighborhoods Revitalization Plan. It also worked to improve refuse collection, housing code enforcement, street sweeping, public safety, and street lighting.

Much of Campus Partners' work focused substantially on the Weinland Park neighborhood. It undertook renovation of section 8 low-income housing, upgraded a three-block commercial strip southeast of campus, and developed some middle-income housing. HUD awarded a COPC grant in 1997 to Campus Collaborative, a multidisciplinary organization of faculty and graduate students from more than forty academic units, founded three years earlier to engage scholars in community issues.[48]

Downtown redevelopment sometimes proceeded with much less controversy. Professional schools of medicine, law, dentistry, pharmacy, and nursing had developed in the nineteenth century in an area near the center of Baltimore. A graduate school opened in the same area in 1917 and a social work school in 1961. Each school had its own facility. In 1970, the legislature combined them into the University of Maryland, Baltimore. In 1992, the university won support from state and city government to rename the area University Center. An advisory committee was charged with creating a sense of campus community and making the area more attractive. In addition to the university, the area houses a major hospital and various other medical facilities. It quickly became an integral part of the city's plan to make downtown Baltimore attractive to residents and tourists. University Center is four blocks from Baltimore's attractive Inner Harbor and just to the north of the Oriole baseball park at Camden Yards.[49]

In 2003, Johns Hopkins University helped to create East Baltimore Development Inc., which successfully relocated, without public protests, a large number of families from the area adjacent to its Medical Center in order to build a Science and Technology Park and new housing. Many other institutions undertook projects in collaboration with local residents. Clark University in Worcester created the University Park Partnership to improve public safety, promote economic development, enhance public education, and increase recreational opportunities for neighborhood residents. Northeastern University in Boston worked with city officials and residents to develop a neighborhood master plan.[50]

In April 2015, looting, fires, and protests broke out in parts of Baltimore after a police officer arrested and seriously injured Freddie Gray, a young black man. In response, a few months later, Johns Hopkins announced a "build, hire, and buy initiative," which provided jobs to local residents and contracts to locally owned small businesses. In making these decisions, Hopkins leaders undoubtedly drew on the experiences of Columbia, Penn, and other institutions.

The Federal Government and Universities in Cities

Urban universities continued to seek federal funds for an urban grant program and continued to cite the land-grant analogy as a precedent. A senior university administrator explained in 1981 that "like the early land-grant colleges which reached into almost every aspect of rural life, the modern urban university is redirecting higher education in the cities."[51] In 1984, Atlanta mayor Andrew Young wrote that "there's a crying out" for universities in cities "to do for urban America what state universities did in the last century for rural America." Like many other elected officials involved in discussions around the urban observatories and the urban grant universities, he believed that "the universities can learn from the cities as much as the cities can learn from the universities."[52] Two years later, *Time* magazine described the unique urban mission of the relatively new University of Massachusetts Boston campus. It quoted Chancellor Robert Corrigan, who characterized his institution as taking "the land-grant concept of service, research, and teaching and bringing it to the urban area . . . to be a force in the community."[53]

In 1993, the University of Illinois at Chicago announced a Great Cities Initiative, committing itself to extensive engagement with its host city in teaching, research, and service programs. It depicted this initiative as implementing the university's "urban land-grant mission."[54] The following year, Peggy Gordon Elliott, former president of the University of Akron, authored a book on *The Urban Campus* published by the American Council on Education. She concluded that "the land-grant institutions have provided an excellent role model" for urban universities. "Like their predecessors . . . the 'asphalt aggies' given half a chance, will lead the way to the 'good society' in the twenty-first century."[55]

The Urban Grant University Act had passed Congress twice, in 1980 and again 1986, but never received funding. In the Clinton administration, however, HUD secretary Henry Cisneros, former mayor of San Antonio, used executive authority to establish an Office of University Partnerships for the department in 1994. That office created a Community Outreach Partnership Centers program (COPC), providing seed money to colleges and universities to help them "reach out to distressed local communities." A HUD report on COPC published in 2000 asserted that "the community partnership role is growing in colleges and universities all across the country," and therefore "colleges and universities are less likely to be seen as 'ivory towers,' but instead as valuable members of the community."[56]

COPC provided funds to support urban university involvement in local revitalization projects, to create a new generation of urban scholars, and to encourage teaching, research, and service partnerships between universities and other federal agencies. The office set up grant programs (1) to establish five-year demonstration centers "to facilitate partnerships between universities and communities to solve urban problems"; (2) to enable historically black colleges and universities to "address local housing, economic development, and neighborhood revitalization needs"; (3) to assist consortia of several institutions to produce "large-scale community building activities"; (4) to fund doctoral research fellowships on subjects "that can influence local and national policymaking"; and (5) to provide work-study support for disadvantaged and minority students enrolled in professional programs in community and economic development.[57]

Cisneros described this initiative as "similar to that underlying one of America's more indigenous ideas in higher education: the land-grant college." He asserted that the nation's higher education institutions "are crucial to the fight to save our cities." But they should participate in rebuilding their communities "not just for moral reasons but also out of enlightened self-interest."[58]

In the program's first eight years, HUD provided $45 million in COPC grants to over a hundred institutions. Public colleges and universities received 77 percent of the grants. Successful applicants had to present evidence that a "genuine partnership" existed between the neighborhood and the academic institution and that neighborhood representatives had joined with university personnel in drafting the proposal.

A study of the program's first three years, commissioned by HUD, found that the partnerships most commonly involved "technical assistance in support of community development, life skills training for community residents, delivery of professional services, particularly health care and legal assistance, information technology, and technical assistance to small businesses" along with other kinds of economic development support. The report noted that universities had used COPC funds to "experiment with integrating teaching and research with other types of outreach activities" and had partnered not only with neighborhood associations and nonprofits but with public schools. Echoing a familiar theme, the report's authors also remarked that community leaders did not understand that universities lacked discretionary funds to pay for neighborhood projects.[59]

The University of California, Los Angeles, received COPC support to research and develop partnerships with community organizations to address inequitable housing and employment conditions in three predominantly black and Hispanic neighborhoods in LA. The University of Illinois at Chicago undertook work with neighborhoods near campus to promote affordable housing, education, and economic development. The University of Minnesota's Center for Urban and Regional Affairs worked with a steering committee in east St. Paul to improve housing, employment and workforce development. The Illinois Institute of Technology helped develop on its campus a charter school for women focused on science and mathematics. Indiana University–Purdue University–Indianapolis assisted the Near Westside neighborhood's efforts to reopen its public high school, which had been closed over vigorous community objections, and to strengthen it once it reopened.

COPC also funded the University of Maryland, Baltimore, to participate in the West Baltimore Empowerment Initiative, providing training in leadership development, community problem-solving, job-readiness centers, and preventive health strategies; the University of Pittsburgh to collaborate with community groups on housing improvement, neighborhood revitalization, job-training education, and youth development; and Duquesne University in Pittsburgh to work with civic organizations in identifying gang members and youth vulnerable to gang recruitment and providing them with education and job opportunities. San Jose State University combined COPC funds and additional funds from the city of San Jose and private foundations to develop an elaborate program for the 360-square-block area surrounding the campus. It assisted area residents with creating small businesses, helping their children succeed in school, developing neighborhood design plans, and it worked with several different city government agencies to determine the most effective use of their resources.[60]

Leaders of major public universities in cities continued efforts to get the federal government to create some version of the urban grant university. In the mid-1990s, a group of thirteen prominent city-based state universities created the Urban 13, changing the name in 1998 to Great Cities' Universities. When the presidents of member institutions met, they discussed ways in which they could form and sustain public-private partnerships to address urban education, housing, environment, criminal justice, transportation, health care, workforce development, and economic growth. Most of the members of the Great Cities' Universities joined the Coalition of Urban Serving Universities (CUSU), created in 2005 to promote public universities in large cities as key agents in addressing urban problems. In 2010, CUSU published a detailed legislative agenda focusing on universities' role in improving the quality of urban teachers and health providers and in strengthening community partnerships. Among its many legislative proposals, it called for establishment of an "'urban grant university' program that designates selected urban universities as leaders in community engagement." Although not a duplicate of the unfunded 1980 urban grant university legislation, it certainly continued the long-standing use of the land-grant analogy by urban universities seeking federal financial support.

CUSU aligned with APLU to jointly promote these programs in Congress. In 2010, Rep. David Wu of Oregon introduced the Urban University Renaissance Act of the Twenty-First Century. The bill incorporated nearly all of CUSU's federal legislative agenda. It included expanded support to HUD for Community Outreach Partnership Centers and authorized funding for higher education institutions to help nonprofit organizations undertake community development and affordable housing projects and improve public education in their cities. It also provided funding to enable early career researchers to pursue work on urban issues. State University of New York chancellor Nancy Zimpher, a leader in CUSU, explained that urban universities had a broad range of skills needed to address the problems of cities, and "federal investment in urban universities" therefore would have great national impact "on strengthening metropolitan prosperity."[61] The enduring idea that universities in cities should research urban problems and use their expertise to work with community groups and the city government remained potent in 2016, as did the belief that the federal government needs to provide funds to major public universities in cities as it did to the land-grant colleges.

Anti-Urbanism and the Definition of "Urban University"

As scholars in major cities' elite universities, and in less selective public and private institutions, actively pursued research on their home cities and worked with city officials to apply their findings to government policy and programs, faculty in all kinds of institutions increasingly sent their students into local communities for internships, research, and public service. Partly as a result of this growing popularity of experiential learning, urban higher education institutions in recent years have become extraordinarily popular among middle-class resident college students. Resident students who are not constrained geographically in their choice of college increasingly prefer to attend institutions in cities so that they can engage in internships and other kinds of activities off campus to enhance their employability upon graduation. Many, having grown up in low density suburban communities, also crave the city's social life.

The revitalization, and gentrification, of major cities like New York, Boston, Chicago, San Francisco, Philadelphia, and many others has also influenced this change. In 2008, Temple University launched its Philadelphia Experience program to link students with the city. It did so, according to the *Chronicle of Higher Education*, because university officials "had been hearing from a growing number of students that Temple's urban location was a major draw." In 1997, 41 percent of new students had told university institutional researchers that its location in a large city was a "very important positive factor" in their choice. By 2007, that figure had increased to 61 percent.[62]

Likewise, in 1992 NYU had received 10,862 applications for freshman admission, and in 2012 there were 43,769 applications. The university's assistant vice president for admissions observed that "whereas 20 years ago the city was our Achilles' heel, it's now our hallmark." She stated that NYU had been able "to leverage its increasingly safe and desirable urban location" to attract many more applicants.[63]

In 2014, a contributing editor of the *Chronicle* highlighted this trend again in an article entitled "Urban Hot Spots Are the Place to Be." He explained that "a college's location might be more important than ever to its long-term prosperity as a residential campus" because most college students seek "hands-on experiences," which are most available in the "vibrant economy" of cities.[64] The following year *Fortune* reported that the American Institute for Economic Research had released a list of the fifteen best large cities in which to attend college to enable prospective students to "weigh the value of their wider community."[65]

Despite these developments, however, when leaders in higher education discussed the needs of "urban university students," they still talked almost exclusively about commuters, minorities, working-class families, working adults, and the "disadvantaged." The new enthusiasm for cities and engaged learning articulated by the leaders of many urban and metropolitan institutions did not change the now widely held belief that enrolling these kinds of students defined what it meant to be an "urban university."

The president of Northeastern Illinois University, discussing the present and future of urban universities in 1981, pointed out that many urban university students attended part-time, came from lower- and middle-class backgrounds, and had the work and family responsibilities of adults. Students at urban universities included a large percentage of "racial and ethnic minorities." These students, he argued, created "a rich and diverse environment" but also presented "a formidable challenge," given their "disparate backgrounds."[66] A Ford Foundation report published in 1983, attested that "in considerable part, the solution to many of the problems of cities depends on educating the people who live and work in them." This job belongs largely to "urban-oriented colleges and universities" whose primary purpose was to educate "working adults, minorities, poor people, persons with low levels of educational preparedness, and increasingly, immigrants whose native language is not English."[67]

In 1985, the College Board released a study of "Today's Urban University Students" based on interviews with students at ten public and private urban colleges and universities. It found that two-thirds of the students did not enroll directly after high school, nearly 30 percent transferred from another institution, most enrolled to enter or advance a career, and a large number worked many hours while attending college. It undertook a case study of students at Hunter College and found that 27 percent were black, 16 percent Hispanic, and 6 percent Asian. One-third were born outside the United States; 40 percent of day students and 28 percent of night students came from families with annual incomes of less than $10,000; 18 percent worked full-time and 41 percent worked part-time. Clearly the College Board researchers did not consider enrollees at universities like NYU, Columbia, Penn, Johns Hopkins, the University of Chicago, and many others "urban university students." Hunter president Donna Shalala, discussing the College Board report's implications, remarked that "at public urban institutions . . . the nontraditional student has become the tradition."[68]

Peggy Gordon Elliott wrote in *The Urban Campus* that "students of the urban era bear almost no resemblance to the image of the student in the fifties." This new majority, she explained, includes many students who must live at home for economic or family reasons or who prefer to live at home and to work while attending college. These students' lives "are more complex" than those of the earlier majority, and therefore "college may not be their number one priority."[69]

Contributors to a 1997 volume on serving students at metropolitan universities wrote almost entirely about how to recruit, retain, and support low-income, part-time, and adult students.[70] And in 2004, Barbara Jacoby published an article in *Metropolitan Universities* on the importance of engaging first-year commuter students. She described how they enter college with educational goals equal to resident students, but they must balance "many competing commitments, including family, work and other responsibilities" and that unlike resident students, commuters tended to work off campus. She expressed concern over the "common misperceptions and myths" about commuters, such as the view that they are "apathetic and uninterested in campus."[71]

Some advocates for the "new majority" urban university student acknowledged that some faculty did not welcome this change. For example, in a book on urban universities, one writer said that faculty must stop viewing "students' motivations and abilities with something bordering on contempt." She urged faculty to understand "what it means to have a student body where sixty percent work full or part time."[72] Likewise, the authors of a 1985 journal article on urban universities called on faculty "to stop living in the past and recognize that circumstances present new challenges."[73]

Debates over open admissions, particularly at New York City's public colleges, continued. In 1994, journalist James Traub published *City on a Hill: Testing the American Dream at City College*, a critique of open admission and remedial instruction. He acknowledged that the creators of open admission saw it as a way of compensating for historic discrimination against black and Puerto Rican students in the educational system. However, open admission "by substituting entitlement for advancement—the achievement of satisfying the rigorous admissions standards of another era—challenges our faith in meritocratic competition and threatens the excellence that the competition made possible."[74]

Governor George Pataki and New York City mayor Rudolph Giuliani declared that CUNY had become vastly inferior to what it had been historically, and they called for toughening standards in the senior institutions. They recruited a new CUNY chancellor, Matthew Goldstein, who initiated an end to open admissions. He also eliminated remedial programs at all of the senior institutions so that students with weak preparation for college initially would have to attend one of CUNY's community colleges.

In July 2000, the *Chronicle of Higher Education* ran a lengthy article on City College, which it described as an institution "that captures the successes and failures of America's urban public universities at helping underprivileged students."[75] The next year, it ran a more upbeat article on Georgia State University. The writer explained that in the past decade, "Georgia State and other urban institutions that lack national stature" had sought to raise their profiles and connect with their alumni. "The typical graduate of an urban institution," he continued, "is more likely to be female, a member of a minority group, and the first family member to attend college" who worked while attending classes and took more than four years to graduate.[76]

Since the 1980s, higher education leaders have spoken with ever-greater enthusiasm about the great assets of their urban locations. New higher education organizations emerged, committed to an urban and metropolitan mission. Service learning and experiential education grew in popularity and became thoroughly mainstream in higher education, increasingly valued as a tool for building civic responsibility among students across the country. Government officials, foundations, journalists, and many others placed great importance on urban research, and more and more social scientists undertook policy-oriented studies of their home cities. Many scholars committed themselves to engaged research, outside of cities as well as within them. The federal government funded programs to engage universities with the research, technical, and educational needs of their cities, and universities worked more closely with local residents in neighborhood improvement projects.

Nonetheless, the "urban university" continued to be understood as a commuter institution educating low-income and minority students and dealing with the victims of urban poverty and racism. Unlike the early twentieth century, when universities in cities had to justify the value of attempting to educate immigrants and working-class citizens, since the 1980s these institutions have been able to point to the extensive educational resources at their fingertips. Deeply engaged in their cities, relatively few of them would call themselves "urban universities," a legacy of the historic anti-urbanism of American higher education.

Conclusion

Change and Continuity

If leaders of American colleges in the late nineteenth century could somehow return to their institutions today, they undoubtedly would be stunned to see how the relationship of colleges and universities to cities changed over the course of the twentieth century. The dramatic urbanization of the United States led to widespread access to post-secondary education for students of all social backgrounds and for working adults. Most students today attend institutions located in cities or metropolitan areas, and most live at home and commute to school. The collegiate ideal of educating young men in the countryside to build character and leadership abilities is long gone.

Those nineteenth-century leaders probably would not be surprised that professional schools, which began largely in cities because of their need to interact with hospitals, courts, government agencies, and the like, remain concentrated in urban areas largely for this reason. So do graduate research and PhD programs inaugurated in the late nineteenth century at new urban institutions like Johns Hopkins University and the University of Chicago. These programs draw heavily on cities' rich resources for research.

They would be amazed, however, to see the many ways baccalaureate education throughout the United States has been molded by the historical experience of urban colleges and universities. City institutions pioneered in what has come to be called the "democratization of higher education." Universities across the country now enroll large numbers of the kinds of "urban students" once viewed with deep skepticism by many academicians. Municipal colleges and other institutions in cities taught commuters, including many adult, part-time, and evening students who could not enroll at traditional residential institutions. Today, commuters of all ages constitute the overwhelming majority of the nation's undergraduate students, and they attend colleges both part-time and full-time across the United States.

Urban colleges also led the way in enrolling students from immigrant families. Now large numbers of immigrants and children of immigrants attend colleges across the country, not just in cities. So do many African American students. Many institutions of higher education offer programs to prepare low-income students to attend and graduate from college, and such programs are widely seen as a key to addressing social and economic inequality in America.

Indeed, the vast majority of students today attend colleges in large metropolitan areas, and many in central cities. One could presume that the extensive presence of commuter, adult, part-time, evening, low-income, immigrant, and African American students is simply an inevitable outgrowth of urbanization. However, historians like to argue that nothing is inevitable until it happens. The democratization of college access for these students has more than a hundred year history, and it is a process that began and expanded in city colleges before spreading to other institutions.

Colleges in cities also pioneered in the now-widespread practice of engaging students and faculty with their surrounding communities. Although most institutions, irrespective of location, now embrace experiential learning and community-engaged scholarship, these practices began in city institutions at the beginning of the twentieth century. Universities in cities today, as they did in the past, offer vastly greater resources for these activities than small-town, rural, and suburban institutions can provide.

In recent years, promoting service learning and community engagement in college has become a national movement aimed at increasing the civic commitment of American citizens. Community engagement and service by college students, the movement's leaders argue, will do a great deal to get young Americans to demonstrate social responsibility. Higher education's enthusiastic embrace of community engagement created several prominent national organizations, including the National Society for Experiential Education, the Council for Adult and Experiential Learning, Campus Compact, and the Coalition of Urban and Metropolitan Universities. It also led the federal government to create agencies like the Corporation for National and Community Service and the Department of Housing and Urban Development's Community Outreach Partnership Center.

This idea of learning in the community also began in city universities. Charles Dabney, in establishing the nation's first cooperative education program in

Cincinnati in 1904, and the other higher educators at urban institutions throughout the twentieth century who joined him in facilitating engagement by urban students, clearly led the way to the widespread embrace of experiential learning in colleges today, both to prepare students for jobs and to build good citizenship.

Urban research and academic programs in urban studies, begun many years ago by universities in cities, now operate in numerous institutions, including colleges and universities not located in urban areas. Some scholars and public officials may still debate whether urban research has been of real value to the cities, but applied research on cities and academic courses and majors in urban affairs are commonplace in social science departments and in other disciplines across the nation. Likewise, research on community needs is no longer limited to urban institutions. The Engagement Scholarship Consortium encourages all universities, not just those in cities, to undertake research of importance to their communities. As efforts to revitalize cities and address the needs of the poor continue, the leaders of these initiatives routinely turn to universities and members of their faculties.

The history of American higher education has been shaped by cities but also by the historical anti-urbanism of American society and its colleges and universities. Flagship state universities employed anti-urbanism to constrain competition from state institutions in cities, creating tensions that continue to this day. More importantly, the deep-seated belief in the collegiate ideal kept city-based institutions on the defensive for many years, as did the "urban crisis" of the 1960s and 1970s. This began to change in the 1990s and the early twenty-first century as knowledge-based employment replaced manufacturing, and as many cities experienced growth in jobs and an increase in upper-middle-class residents, particularly young adults. Baccalaureate programs in cities became increasingly appealing to prospective residential students, creating a problem for some small-town and rural liberal arts colleges in attracting applicants.

Does this mean that anti-urbanism has disappeared in American higher education? It certainly has modified the classic view of urban universities as institutions defined by their low-income, commuter, and minority students. Whether the term "urban university" still evokes that image among significant numbers of faculty, students, administrators, and others is hard to know. There is no question, however, that anti-urbanism profoundly shaped higher education in cities, and that higher education in cities profoundly shaped contemporary American higher education.

Notes

CHAPTER ONE: The Collegiate Ideal and Nineteenth-Century Cities

1. Charles F. Thwing, *American Colleges: Their Students and Work*, 2nd ed. (New York: P. G. Putnam, 1883), 44–46.

2. Mark I. Gelfand, *A Nation of Cities: The Federal Government and Urban America, 1933–1965* (Oxford: Oxford University Press, 1975), 72–74.

3. Quoted in Charles N. Glaab and A. Theodore Brown, *A History of Urban America*, 3rd ed. (New York: Macmillan, 1983), 53, 56, 113.

4. Josiah Strong, *Our Country: Its Possible Future and Its Present Crisis* (New York: Baker & Taylor for the American Home Missionary Society, 1885), 129.

5. Steven Conn, *Americans against the City: Anti-urbanism in the Twentieth Century* (Oxford: Oxford University Press, 2014), chap. 1.

6. Roy Rosenzweig and Elizabeth Blackmar, *The Park and the People: A History of Central Park* (New York: Henry Holt, 1994), 22–30.

7. Ellen Stroud, *Nature Next Door: Cities and Trees in the American Northeast* (Seattle: University of Washington Press, 2012); Galen Cranz, *The Politics of Park Design: A History of Urban Parks in America* (Cambridge, MA: MIT Press, 1982).

8. L. A. Dunn, *Review of the History of the American College with Reference to Location* (Pella, IA: A. T. Betzer, 1976), 28.

9. Frederick Rudolph, *The American College and University: A History* (New York: Knopf, 1965), chap. 5.

10. Roger Geiger, *The History of American Higher Education: Learning and Culture from the Founding to World War II* (Princeton, NJ: Princeton University Press, 2015), 411.

11. Helen Lefkowitz Horowitz, *Alma Mater: Design and Experience in the Women's Colleges from Their Nineteenth-Century Beginnings to the 1930s* (New York: Knopf, 1984), 3–7.

12. Robert A. McCaughey, *Stand, Columbia: A History of Columbia University in the City of New York, 1875–2004* (New York: Columbia University Press, 2004), chap. 1.

13. Theodore Francis Jones, *New York University, 1932–1932* (New York: New York University Press, 1933); Henry MacCracken, "A Metropolitan University: A Speech Delivered before the Nineteenth Century Club," *The Christian at Work*, May 5–11, 1892, 24.

14. Quoted in C. H. Cramer, *Case Western Reserve: A History of the University, 1826–1876* (Boston: Little, Brown, 1976), 7.

15. Charles Franklin Thwing, *The American College in American Life* (New York: G. P. Putnam's Sons, 1897).

16. Kathleen Kilgore, *Transformations: A History of Boston University* (Boston: Boston University, 1991), 41

17. Quoted in Bill Carey, *Chancellors, Commodores, and Coeds: A History of Vanderbilt University* (Nashville, TN: Clearbrook Press, 2003).

18. Ridgely Torrence, *The Story of John Hope* (New York: Macmillan, 1948), 108.

19. Joe Martin Richardson, *A History of Fisk University* (Tuscaloosa: University of Alabama Press, 1980), 3, 41.

20. Benjamin Brawley, *History of Morehouse College* (College Park, MD: McGrath, 1917), 9–10; Edward A. Jones, *A Candle in the Dark: A History of Morehouse College* (Valley Forge, PA: Judson Press, 1967), 37–39, 62–63.

21. Rayford Logan, *Howard University: The First Hundred Years, 1867–1967* (New York: NYU Press, 1969), 26–28; Walter Dyson, *Howard University: The Capstone of Negro Education, 1867–1940* (Washington, DC: Howard University, 1941).

22. Quoted in William Kinnison, *Building Sullivant's Pyramid: An Administrative History of Ohio State University, 1870–1907* (Columbus: Ohio State University Press, 1970), 41.

23. James W. Fraser, *Preparing America's Teachers: A History* (New York: Teachers College Press, 2007), 154–64.

24. Christine A. Ogren, *The American State Normal School: "An Instrument of Great Good"* (New York: Palgrave Macmillan, 2005), 213–35.

25. Walter H. Hill, *Historical Sketch of the St. Louis University: The Commemoration of its Fiftieth Anniversary or Golden Jubilee, on June 24, 1879* (St. Louis: Patrick Fox, 1879), 54, 99.

26. Quoted in Lee J. Bennish, *Continuity and Change: Xavier University, 1931–1981* (Chicago: Loyola University Press, 1981), 95.

27. Anthony Kuzniewski, *Thy Honored Name: A History of the College of the Holy Cross, 1943–1994* (Washington, DC: Catholic University Press, 1999), 20–29.

28. Charles F. Donovan, David Dunigan, and Paul A, Fitzgerald, *History of Boston College: From the Beginnings to 1990* (Chestnut Hill, MA: University Press of Boston College, 1990), 115–18.

29. David Starr Jordan, *The Voice of the Scholar* (San Francisco: Paul Elder, 1903), 229.

30. John Thelin, *A History of American Higher Education*, 2nd ed. (Baltimore: Johns Hopkins University Press, 2011), 53–55.

31. Roger G. Geiger, *The History of American Higher Education: Learning and Culture from the Founding to World War II* (Princeton, NJ: Princeton University Press, 2015), 385.

32. Edward Pitts Cheyney, *History of the University of Pennsylvania, 1740–1940* (New York: Arno, 1977), 208.

CHAPTER TWO: Urban Reality, 1900–1945

1. Parke Rexford Kolbe, *Urban Influences on Higher Education in England and the United States* (New York: Macmillan, 1928), 241–44.

2. Charles N. Glaab and A. Theodore Brown, *A History of Urban America*, 3rd ed. (New York: Macmillan, 1983), 125.

3. Gail Radford, *The Rise of Public Authority: Statebuilding and Economic Development in Twentieth-Century America* (Chicago: University of Chicago Press, 2013), chap. 3.

4. Steven Conn, *Americans against the City: Anti-urbanism in the Twentieth Century* (Oxford: Oxford University Press, 2014), chap. 2 and 3; Lisa Krissoff Boehm and Steven H. Corey, *America's Urban History* (New York: Routledge, 2015), chap. 5; Glaab and Brown, *History of Urban America*, chap. 12.

5. Quoted in Roger Biles, *The Fate of Cities: Urban America and the Federal Government, 1946–2000* (Lawrence: University Press of Kansas, 2011), 6.

6. Mark Gelfand, *Nation of Cities: The Federal Government and Urban America, 1933–1965* (Oxford: Oxford University Press, 1975), chap. 3.

7. Harold S. Wechsler, "Brewing Bachelors: The History of the University of Newark," *Paedgogica Historica* 46, no. 1–2 (February–April 2010): 232.

8. Richard McCormick, *Rutgers: A Bicentennial History* (New Brunswick, NJ: Rutgers University Press, 1966), 243–44.

9. William E. Terry, *Origin and Development of Texas Southern University, Houston, Texas* (Houston: W. E. Terry, 1978), 107–8.

10. Arthur Lefevre, *The Organization and Administration of a State's Institutions of Higher Education* (Austin, TX: Von Boeckmann-Jones, 1914), 149.

11. George Barton Cutten, "A Small Community as a College Site," *New York Times*, July 27, 1930.

12. George Zook, "Is the Junior College a Menace or a Boon," *School Review* 37, no. 6 (June 1929): 415.

13. John Huston Finley, "The University and the City," *Journal of Higher Education* 3, no. 5 (May 1932): 230.

14. David Hollinger, "Two NYUs and the Obligations of Universities to the Social Order in the Great Depression," in *The University and the City: From Medieval Origins to the Present*, ed. Thomas Bender (New York: Oxford University Press, 1988), 255.

15. R. H. Eckelberry, *The History of the Municipal University in the United States* (Washington, DC: Office of Education, US Department of the Interior, GPO, 1932), 169–70.

16. "The Municipal University as a Civic Investment," *Current Opinion* 59, no. 5 (November 1915): 341.

17. James N. Crooks, "The AUU and the Mission of the Urban University," *Urbanism Past and Present* 7, no. 14 (1982): 34–39; Thomas Arthur Kaluzynski, "An Historical View of the Concept of an Urban University" (PhD thesis, University of Illinois at Urbana-Champaign, 1975), 50.

18. Elizabeth Hoey, "A College Grows in Brooklyn," in *St. Francis College: The First One Hundred Years*, ed. Christopher Florentz (Brooklyn: St. Francis College, 1984), 107.

19. James M. Lee, "Professor James Melvin Lee Discusses Working One's Way through College," *New York Times*, February 2, 1913.

20. "Urban College Men to Meet Thursday," *New York Times*, November 11, 1928; "N.Y.U. Dean Hails the Urban College," *New York Times*, December 16, 1928.

21. Charles Dabney, "The Municipal University," in *Summary of the Proceedings of the First Session of the National Association of Municipal Universities* (Washington, DC: US Bureau of Education, 1915), 7–10.

22. Gene D. Lewis and Zane L. Miller, "Charles W. Dabney and the Urban University: An Institution in Search of a Mission," *Cincinnati Historical Society Bulletin* 38, no. 3 (1980): 151–78; Charles William Dabney, "The University and the City in Co-operation," *Outlook* 89, no. 13 (July 25, 1908): 655–71; John L. Patterson, "Municipal Universities of the United States," *National Municipal Review* 5 (October 1916): 558.

23. Patterson, "Municipal Universities," 553–64.

24. "NYU Dean Hails the Urban College," *New York Times*, December 16, 1928.

25. Clyde Lyndon King, "Co-operation Between Universities and Cities," *National Municipal Review* 5 (January 1916): 122–23.

26. A. Monroe Stowe, "A Modern American College" (typescript history of the University of Toledo, 1927), 2.

27. *Proceedings of the Annual Meeting of the Association of Urban Universities* 26 (1939): 39 (hereafter cited as *AUU Proceedings*).

28. Edward A. Fitzpatrick, "The University and the City," *School and Society* 49 (January 14, 1939), 42.

29. Walton John, "Distinguishing Urban Universities," *School Life* 23, no. 1 (September 1937): 20.

30. *AUU Proceedings* 14 (1927): 23–24.

31. *AAU Proceedings* 14 (1927): 76–77; 20 (1933): 31.

32. William Tufant Foster, "Should Students Study?," *Harper's Monthly* 133 (1916): 612. The article was included also in his 1917 book of the same title, published by Harper and Brothers.

33. Archibald L. Bouton, *The Colleges and Americanism* (n.p.: n.p., 1919); Robert Shaffer, "Jews, Reds, and Violets: Anti-Semitism and Anti-Radicalism at New York University, 1916–1929," *Journal of Ethnic Studies* 15, no. 2 (1987): 59–60, 66–67.

34. George Davis, "Address to Graduates," George Davis Collection, box 1, folder 5, Hunter College Archives, New York.

35. "Address to be Delivered by Dr. Eugene Colligan, November 30, 1936," Eugene Colligan Collection, box 2, folder 7, Hunter College Archives, New York.

36. George H. Shuster, *The Ground I Walked On* (New York: Farrar, Straus & Cudahy, 1961), 104; Katherina Kroo Grunfeld, "Purpose and Ambiguity: The Feminine World of Hunter College, 1869–1945" (EdD diss., Teachers College, Columbia University, 1991), 205–7, 217–18.

37. "Free City Colleges to Bar Aliens under Ruling Based on 1926 Law," *New York Times*, February 3, 1938; "City's Colleges Remove Ban on Alien Students," *New York Herald Tribune*, August 4, 1938.

38. Wechsler, "Brewing Bachelors," 237–41.

39. "Spiritual Revival in Colleges Urged," *New York Times*, October 24, 1939, 16.

40. Quoted in Nathan Glazer, "City College," in *Academic Transformation: Seventeen Institutions under Pressure*, ed. David Riesman and Verne A. Stadtman (New York: McGraw-Hill, 1973).

41. Quoted in Harold S. Wechsler, "One-Third of a Campus: Ruth Crawford Mitchell and Second-Generation Americans at the University of Pittsburgh," *History of Education Quarterly* 48, no. 1 (February 2008): 97–98, 103.

42. *AUU Proceedings* 31 (1944): 15; Wechsler, "One-Third of a Campus," 119–22. See also "Training to Win: Inside the Cathedral of Learning" (brochure, University of Pittsburgh, n.d.).

43. *AUU Proceedings* 5 (1920): 99.

44. Kolbe, *Urban Influences on Higher Education*, 127.

45. *AUU Proceedings* 14 (1927): 77.

46. *AUU Proceedings* 15 (1928): 9.

47. *AUU Proceedings* 20 (1933): 44.

48. *AUU Proceedings* 22 (1935): 55.

49. Ibid., 54.

50. "The Relation of the University to the Community," *Education* 32 (January 1912): 316.

51. Charles F. Thwing, *The College Gateway* (Boston: Pilgrim Press, 1918), 162–64.

52. John L. Patterson, "Municipal Universities of the United States," *National Municipal Review* 5 (October 1916): 553–64.

53. Charles F. Donovan, David Dunigan, and Paul A, Fitzgerald, *History of Boston College from the Beginnings to 1940* (Chestnut Hill, MA: University Press of Boston College, 1990); Lee J. Bennish, *Continuity and Change: Xavier University, 1831–1981* (Chicago: Loyola University Press, 1981), 95; Herman J. Muller, *The University of Detroit, 1977–1977: A Centennial History* (Detroit: University of Detroit, 1976), 77.

54. John Dyer, *The Ivory Tower in the Market Place: The Evening College in American Education* (Indianapolis, Ind.: Bobbs-Merrill, 1956), 37–38.

55. *AUU Proceedings* 16–17 (1929/30): 15, 153.

56. *The Obligations of Universities to the Social Order: Addresses and Discussion at a Conference of Universities* (New York: NYU Press, 1933), 27.

57. *AUU Proceedings* 28 (1941): 59–60.

58. Carnegie Corporation of New York Archives, series IIIA (Grants), box 272, University of Newark folder, Columbia University Rare Book and Manuscript Library, New York.

59. Herbert Sorenson, *Adult Abilities in Extension Classes* (Minneapolis: University of Minnesota Press, 1933) and *Adult Abilities: A Study of University Extension Students* (Minneapolis: University of Minnesota Press, 1938); Earl J. McGrath, "College Aptitude of Adult Students," *University of Buffalo Studies* 14, no. 1 (November 1936): 32.

60. McGrath, "College Aptitude of Adult Students," 76–77.

61. Charles Bulger, "The Industrial Worker as a College Student," *School and Society* 11 (February 28, 1920): 266.

62. National Resources Committee, *Supplementary Report of the Urbanism Committee, vol. I: Urban Government* (Washington, DC: GPO, 1939/40), 182; Harry H. Freeman, *Twenty Years of Municipal Research: A Discussion of the Municipal Research Movement in America* (New York: Governmental Research Association, 1926), 4–8.

63. Edward Fitzpatrick, "University Training for Public Service," *American Political Science Review* 8, no. 4 (November 1914): 674, "Universities and Training for Public Service," *Survey* 32 (September 19, 1914): 614–15; "An Institute of Political and Administrative Research," *School and Society* 3, no. 64 (March 25, 1916): 449–52.

64. Charles A. Beard, "Training for Efficient Public Service," *Annals of the American Academy of Political and Social Science* 64 (March 1916): 218, 221.

65. Hindy Lauer Schachter, "When Political Science Championed Public Service Training: The American Political Science Association Campaign for Professional Public Administration," *American Review of Public Administration* 37 (2007): 362–68; William Bennett Munro, "Instruction in Municipal Government in the Universities and Colleges of the United States," *National Municipal Review* 2 (July 1913): 425–38.

66. James Heaton, "A School for Mayors," *Survey* 27 (December 9, 1911): 1340–41.

67. Herman G. James, "The City's Need, the University's Opportunity," *American City* 10 (March 1914): 247–49.

68. "The California Bureau of Municipal Reference," *American City* 9 (November 1913): 401–2.

69. Jeremiah W. Jenks, "Co-operation between City Governments and Universities," *National Municipal Review* 3, no. 4 (October 1914): 764–66.

70. Edwin A. Cottrell, "The Municipal Service of the University," *Ohio State University Bulletin* 22, no. 34 (May 1918): 327.

71. Morris Llewellyn Cooke, *Our Cities Awake: Notes on Municipal Activities and Administration* (New York: Doubleday, Page, 1918), 150.

72. Schachter, "When Political Science Championed Public Service Training," 369.

73. Theodore Francis Jones, ed., *New York University, 1832–1932* (New York: New York University Press, 1933), 341–45.

74. Julian Park, "The City and the University," *University of Buffalo Studies* 1, no. 2 (June 1920): 195, quoted in John Puckett and Mark Frazier Lloyd, *Becoming Penn: The Pragmatic American University, 1950–2000* (Philadelphia: University of Pennsylvania Press, 2015), 93; Lewis and Miller, "Charles W. Dabney," 164.

75. Steven Diner, *A City and Its Universities: Public Policy in Chicago, 1892–1919* (Chapel Hill: University of North Carolina Press, 1980); John Louis Recchiuti, *Civic Engagement: Social Science and Progressive Era Reform in New York* (Philadelphia: University of Pennsylvania Press, 2007); "Brown University Development of Community Program in Fine Arts," in Carnegie Corporation Archives, series IIIA (Grants), box 65.

76. Dabney, "University and the City in Co-operation," 665, and "The Municipal University and Its Work," *Addresses and Proceedings: National Education Association of the United States* 50 (July 6–12, 1912): 774.

77. Charles H. Levermore, "A Complete Municipal University," *North American Review* 196, no. 5 (November 1912): 712.

78. *Catholic World* 65 (September 1897): 861–62.

79. Thomas Jablonsky, *Milwaukee's Jesuit University: Marquette, 1881–1981* (Milwaukee: Marquette University Press, 2007), 133–34; *Marquette's Silver Jubilee: A Memoir, 1881–1906* (Milwaukee: Marquette University, 1906).

CHAPTER THREE: Postwar Higher Education and the Needs of Cities, 1945–1963

1. Roger Biles, *The Fate of Cities: Urban America and the Federal Government, 1946–2000* (Lawrence: University Press of Kansas, 2011), 82.

2. James Gregory, "The Second Great Migration: An Historical Overview," in Kenneth L. Kusmer and Joe W. Trotter, eds., *African American Urban History Since World War II* (University of Chicago Press, 2009), 19–38.

3. Steven Conn, *Americans against the City: Anti-urbanism in the Twentieth Century* (Oxford: Oxford University Press, 2014), 157.

4. Quoted in Biles, *Fate of Cities*, 99.

5. Dongbin Kim and John L. Rury, "The Changing Profile of College Access: The Truman Commission and Enrollment Patterns in the Postwar Era," *History of Education Quarterly* 47, no. 3 (August 2007): 302–27; Martin Trow, "The Democratization of Higher Education in America," *European Journal of Sociology* 3, no. 2 (1962): 231–62.

6. Joseph Hudnut, *Blueprint for a University* (Detroit: Wayne University Press, 1944), 5–6.

7. Samuel P. Capen, "Academic Frontiers: The Growth of the University of Buffalo," in *Centennial Celebration of the University of Buffalo, 1846–1946* (Buffalo, NY: n.p., 1946), 15.

8. *Proceedings of the Annual Meeting of the Association of Urban Universities* 36 (1949): 80–87 (hereafter cited as *AUU Proceedings*).

9. *AUU Newsletter* 8, no. 1 (January 1956): 3.

10. *AUU Proceedings* 46 (1959): 14.

11. *AUU Proceedings* 49 (1962): 61.

12. William Carlson, *The Municipal University* (Washington, DC: Center for Applied Research in Education, 1962), 36–38.

13. *AUU Proceedings* 33 (1946): 103; Ordway Tead, "The Extracurricular Challenges in Urban Universities," *School and Society* 65, no. 1685 (April 12, 1947): 257.

14. "Educator Upholds Ivy-Clad Colleges," *New York Times*, December 3, 1946.

15. *AUU Proceedings* 36 (1949): 54.

16. *AUU Proceedings* 38 (1951): 85.

17. *AUU Proceedings* 39 (1952): 50–56.

18. Thomas Evans Coulton, *A City College in Action: Struggle and Achievement at Brooklyn College, 1930–1955* (New York: Harper & Brothers, 1955), 14.

19. *AUU Proceedings* 46 (1959): 14–15.

20. Milton Katz, "A New Step in the President's Program: The Urban University, July 22, 1958," and "Elements of a possible program for a selected urban university" (draft memo), Ford Foundation Records, Catalogued Reports (FA739), box 424, report 10468, Rockefeller Archive Center, Sleepy Hollow, NY.

21. Martin Trow, "The Democratization of Higher Education in America," *European Journal of Sociology* 3, 2 (1962): 245; David Boroff, "The Case for the Asphalt Campus: A search for 'maturity' weighs the choice between town and country college, *New York Times*, April 21, 1963: 83.

22. John K. Folger, "Urban Sprawl in the Academic Community: Alleviating the University's Growing Pains," *Journal of Higher Education*, vol. 34. no. 8 (Nov, 1963): 450–57.

23. Monikaq Kehoe and Ray Margaret Lawrence, "The Personnel Advisor in a City College," *Journal of Higher Education* 16, no. 3 (March 1945): 141–46.

24. Ruth O. McCarn and Margaret Blair, "Advising the Commuting Student," in *Counseling and Guidance in General Education*, ed. Melvene Hardee (Yonkers, NY: World Book, 1955), 272–74.

25. *AUU Proceedings* 50 (1963): 28.

26. "Foundation Resolution: Columbia University Institute for Urban Land Use and Housing Studies" (February 20, 1948), Rockefeller Foundation Archives, RG 1.2, series 200S, box 492, folder 4205, Rockefeller Archive Center.

27. Interview record, June 20, 1951, Carnegie Corporation of New York Archives, series III.A (Grants), box 288, 2, Columbia University Rare Book and Manuscript Library, New York.

28. "The History of City Planning and Landscape Design: A Summary Report to the Rockefeller Foundation, 1956–1958, April 23, 1958 " Rockefeller Foundation Archives, RG 1.2, series 200R.

29. "Grant to the New School for Social Research for a study by Mrs. Jane Jacobs of relations of function to design in large cities" (September 8, 1958), Rockefeller Foundation Archives, RG 1.2, series 200R, box 390, folders 3380–81.

30. Carnegie Corporation Archives, Series III.A (Grants), box 103; Rockefeller Foundation Archives, RG 1.2 (FA387), series 200: US, Subseries 200R, Box 310, City College Metropolitan Area Study.

31. Carnegie Corporation Archives, Series III.A (Grants), box 70.

32. Robert Gutman and David Popence, eds., "Urban Studies: Present Trends and Future Prospects in an Emerging Academic Field," special issue of *American Behavioral Scientist* 6, no. 6 (February 1963): 11, 17, 62.

33. Jack H. Vaughn, "Urban Crisis and Academe," *College and University Journal* 10, no. 3 (May 1971): 17–19.

34. *AUU Proceedings* 45 (1958): 46–47, 57–59.

35. Ford Foundation Records, Projects (FA733), C-520, reel no. 83.

36. Charles G. Dobbins, ed., *The University, the City, and Urban Renewal: Report of a Regional Conference Sponsored by the American Council on Education and the West Philadelphia Corporation Philadelphia, March 25, 1963* (Washington, DC: ACE, 1964); Committee on Urban Renewal, American Council on Education Records, box 578, folder 18, Hoover Institution Library and Archives, Stanford, CA.

37. Special Committee on Urban Renewal, American Council on Education Records, box 440, folder 4; box 497, folder 17; and box 579, folder 18; Educational Facilities Laboratory, *Campus in the City* (New York: n.p., 1968), 2–3.

38. Housing and Home Finance Agency, *18th Annual Report, 1964* (Washington, DC: GPO, 1965), 326.

39. Michael Carriere, "Chicago, the South Side Planning Board, and the Search for (Further) Order: Toward an Intellectual Lineage of Urban Renewal in Postwar America," *Journal of Urban History* 39, no. 3 (May 2013): 411–32.

40. Julian Levi, *The Neighborhood Program of the University of Chicago* (Chicago: n.p., August 1961); David B. Carlson, "Town and Gown," *Architectural Forum* 118 (March 1963): 93–94; George Nash and Patricia Nash, *Leads Columbia Could Have Followed* (New York: Columbia University Bureau of Applied Social Research, June 3, 1968), 38; LaDale Winling, "Students and the Second Ghetto: Federal Legislation, Urban Politics, and Campus Planning at the University of Chicago," *Journal of Planning History* 10, no. 1 (2011): 59–86; Davarian L. Baldwin, "The '800-Pound Gargoyle': The Long History of Higher Education and Urban Development on Chicago's South Side," *American Quarterly* 67, no. 1 (March 2015): 87.

41. Kermit Parsons, "A Truce in the War between Universities and Cities: A Prologue to the Study of University-Community Relations," *Journal of Higher Education* 34, no. 1 (January 1963): 24, 25; Robert A. McCaughey, *Stand, Columbia: A History of Columbia University in the City of New York, 1974–2004* (New York: Columbia University Press, 2003), 404–7; Themis Chronopoulos, *Spatial Regulation in New York City: From Urban Renewal to Zero Tolerance* (New York: Routledge, 2011), 42–55.

42. Michael Carriere, "Fighting the War against Blight: Columbia University, Morningside Heights, Inc., and Counterinsurgent Urban Renewal," *Journal of Planning History* 10, no. 1 (2011): 5–12.

43. Quoted in John Puckett and Mark Frazier Lloyd, *Becoming Penn: The Pragmatic American University, 1950–2000* (Philadelphia: University of Pennsylvania Press, 2015), 93.

44. Nash and Nash, *Leads Columbia Could Have Followed*, 40–41; George Nash and Patricia Nash, *Survey of Activities in Urban and Minority Problems at the University of Pennsylvania* (New York: Columbia University Planning Committee, 1967); Gaylord P. Harnwell, "The University and the Rehabilitation of the Central City," *AUU Proceedings* 47 (1960): 18–21; Ira Harkavy and John L. Puckett, "The Role of Mediating Structures in University and Community Revitalization: The University of Pennsylvania and West Philadelphia as a Case Study," *Journal of Research and Development in Education* 25, no. 1 (Fall 1991): 16; Harley F. Etienne, *Pushing Back the Gates: Neighborhood Perspectives on University-Driven Revitalization in West Philadelphia* (Philadelphia: Temple University Press, 2012), 18; Dobbins, *University, the City, and Urban Renewal.*

45. Robert L. Carroll, Hayden B. May, and Samuel V. Noe, *University-Community Tension and Urban Community Form* (Cincinnati, OH: University of Cincinnati, 1972), 1:44–49.

46. J. Mark Souther, "Acropolis of the Middle-West: Decay, Renewal, and Boosterism in Cleveland's University Circle," *Journal of Planning History* 10, no. 1 (2011): 30–58; *AUU Proceedings* 43 (1956): 14–17; Kermit Parsons, "Universities and Cities: The Terms of the Truce between Them," *Journal of Higher Education* 34, no. 4 (April 1963): 212–14; "Cleveland's University Circle Area," Ford Foundation Records, Projects (FA733), C-439, reel p-1010.

47. Deborah Caruso Marrone, *Fordham University and the United States: A History* (New York: E-Lit Books, 2013), 152–55.

48. "Universities, Colleges Operate as a Major Force in Local Renewal Programs," *Journal of Housing* 19, no. 1 (January 1962): 503–11.

49. Ibid., 503.

50. John R. Thelin, *A History of American Higher Education*, 2nd ed. (Baltimore: Johns Hopkins University Press, 2011), 206–7; Margaret Cheney and Patricia A. Pelfrey, *A Brief History of the University of California*, 2nd ed. (Berkeley: University of California Press, 2004).

51. George Rosen, *Decision-Making Chicago Style: The Genesis of a University of Illinois Campus* (Urbana: University of Illinois Press, 1980); Fred W. Beuttler, "Envisioning and Urban University: President David Henry and the Chicago Circle Campus of the University of Illinois, 1955–1975," *History of Higher Education Annual* 23 (2003/4): 107–41.

52. J. Martin Klotsche, *The University of Wisconsin–Milwaukee: An Urban University* (Milwaukee: University of Wisconsin–Milwaukee, 1972), 25.

53. Ibid., 25–29, 30–31, 60–61.

54. Richard M. Freeland, *Academia's Golden Age: Universities in Massachusetts, 1945–1970* (Oxford: Oxford University Press, 1992), chap. 6.

55. Harold S. Wechsler, "Brewing Bachelors: The History of the University of Newark," *Paedgogica Historica* 46, no. 1–2 (February–April 2010): 47.

CHAPTER FOUR: Response to the Urban Crisis, 1964–1980

1. Roger Biles, *Fate of Cities: Urban America and the Federal Government, 1946–2000* (Lawrence: University Press of Kansas, 2011), 202; Lisa Krissoff Boehm and Steven J. Corey, *America's Urban History* (New York: Routledge, 2015), 297–98.

2. John F. Bauman, Roger Biles, and Kristin M. Szylvian, *The Ever-Changing American City: 1945–Present* (Lanham, MD: Rowman & Littlefield, 2012), 96.

3. Ibid., 95.

4. *Proceedings of the Annual Meeting of the Association of Urban Universities* 51 (1964): 17 (hereafter cited as *AUU Proceedings*).

5. "Higher Education for Urban America," special supplement to *Educational Record* 46 (Summer 1965): 303.

6. Sanford L. Kravitz, "Urban Institutions as University Clients," in *Political Backgrounds of Adult Education: The University in Urban Society*, ed. Thomas Cummings Jr. (Boston: Boston University Center for the Study of Liberal Education, 1967), 23.

7. Roger W. Axford, ed., *College-Community Consultation* (DeKalb: Northern Illinois University, College of Continuing Education, 1967), 1.

8. *The Vitality of the City: A Challenge to Higher Education* (San Francisco: University of California, San Francisco Medical Center, 1967), 35.

9. Byron Johnson, "Challenge to Education: A New Approach," in ibid., 49.

10. "Town and Gown: The Urban Community and the University," *Bulletin of the American Academy of Arts and Sciences* 22, no. 6 (April 1969): 2–10.

11. David C. Nichols and Olive Mills, eds., *The Campus and the Racial Crisis* (Washington, DC: American Council on Education, 1970); G. M. Sawyer, "The Urban University: Toward Harmony or Hiatus," presented at the conference on "The Urban Involvement of Higher Education in the 1970s," March 1974, American Council on Education (ACE) Archives, box 705, folder 5, Hoover Institution Archives, Stanford, CA.

12. Martin Jenkins and Bernard Ross, *The Urban Involvement of Higher Education in the 1970s: Summary of Four 1974 Regional Conferences* (Washington, DC: US Department of Housing & Urban Development, 1974): 1.

13. Eric Cox, "The University and the Decaying American City," *Educational Record* 45, no. 4 (Fall 1964): 395–400.

14. Paul Reinert, *The Urban Catholic University* (New York: Sheed & Ward, 1970), 102, 120.

15. David E. Sumner, *Urban Universities and the City* (Washington, DC: Eric Clearinghouse on Higher Education, April 1970), 2.

16. Quoted in Catherine A. Connor, "'The University That Ate Birmingham': The Healthcare Industry, Urban Development, and Neoliberalism," *Journal of Urban History* 42, no. 2 (March 2016): 288.

17. Martin Jenkins, *The Urban Affairs Programs of Higher Education Associations: What They Are Doing and What They Can Do* (ACE Special Report, October 1971); Jeffrey E. Dutton and Martin D. Jenkins, "The Urban Involvement of Colleges and Universities," *Higher Education Panel Report, American Council on Education*, Survey no. 15 (Washington, DC: HUD, August 24, 1973).

18. "For the Urban University," *New York Times*, June 30, 1964.

19. "Universities Told of Chance to Help Urban Revolution," *New York Times*, December 27, 1966.

20. "Abrams Urges Urban Colleges to Give Communities More Aid," *New York Times*, September 25, 1968.

21. Glen C. Pulver, Daniel J. Schler, and Lee J. Cary, *The Role of the University in Community Development* (Columbia: University of Missouri Urban Extension Division, 1969), 25.

22. *The Urban University and the Urban Community* (Boston: Boston University Metrocenter, n.d.), 2:1.

23. William Birenbaum, "Cities and Universities: Collision of Crises," in *Campus 1980*, ed. Alvin C. Eurich (New York: Delacorte, 1968), 58; William Birenbaum, *Overlive: Power, Poverty, and the University* (New York: Delacorte, 1969), 194.

24. Quoted in Birenbaum, *Overlive*, 194.

25. *AUU Proceedings* 55 (1967): 43.

26. Kevin White, "The View from City Hall," in "Confrontation: The Campus and the City," special issue of *Change in Higher Education* 1, no. 1 (January/February 1969): 7.

27. Eldon L. Johnson, "The Urban Outreach Problems of Research Universities," paper presented at "The Urban Involvement of Higher Education in the 1970s," March 1974, ACE Archives, box 705, folder 4.

28. Joseph G. Coleman, "Higher Education and the City in the Seventies" (presented at the National Seminar on the University in Community Service, University of Maryland, October 2, 1968), 7–8; Harr quote, 12.

29. Howard Mitchell, ed., *The University and the Urban Crisis* (New York: Behavioral Publications, 1974), 11.

30. Leonard Duhl, "Effecting Social Change," in *Universities and Foundations: Search for Relevance*, ed. Werner Z. Hirsch (Los Angeles: UCLA Institute of Government and Public Affairs, 1968), 17.

31. "U. of Minnesota Weighs Urban-Affairs Role," *New York Times*, February 27, 1966; Fran P. Hoskin, "Topics: The Future of the Urban University," *New York Times*, September 10, 1966.

32. *Urban University and the Urban Community*, 3:1.

33. Glenn Tinder, "Incipient Catastrophe: The University and the City," *Massachusetts Review* 8, no. 3 (Summer 1967): 491–92.

34. Roald F. Campbell, "Higher Education and the Demand for Social Action" (presented at the American Association for Higher Education's 24th National Conference on Higher Education, Chicago, March 3, 1969), 2–3.

35. Colin Greer, "The Issues and the Stakes," in "Confrontation: The Campus and the City," 15.

36. Harold Enarson, "Higher Education and Community Services," in Nichols and Mills, *Campus and the Racial Crisis*, 245.

37. Warren G. Bennis, "The Role of the University in Restoring the Urban Habitat," *Educational Record*, Fall 1974, 223.

38. Malcolm Moos, "The Far Side of the Urban University," Ford Foundation Records, Program Management Cost Files (FA501), series III, E&R—FY 1977 Administrative File—Malcolm Moos Consultancy on the Urban University (MCA 77-980), 1976–1977, Rockefeller Archive Center, Sleepy Hollow, NY.

39. Ernest Spaights, "Toward a Definition of an Urban University," *Urban Education* 15, no. 3 (October 1980): 369–74.

40. *AUU Proceedings* 50 (1963): vii.

41. *AUU Proceedings* 55 (1968): 19.

42. Coleman, "Higher Education and the City," 9.

43. Leonard E. Goodall, "The Urban University: Is There Such a Thing?," *Journal of Higher Education* 41, no. 1 (January 1970): 48.

44. Ira B. Bryant, *Texas Southern University: Its Antecedents, Political Origin and Future* (Houston: Ira B. Bryant, 1975), chap. 8.

45. Maurice Berube, *The Urban University in America* (Westport, CT: Greenwood, 1978), 14.

46. Spaights, "Toward a Definition," 369.

47. *AUU Proceedings* 58 (1972): 25.

48. "Instructions and Guidelines for Consultants" (memo), February 8, 1978, Ford Foundation Records, Education and Research Division, Office Files of Fred E. Crossland (FA713), series I, subseries E: Urban Universities.

49. James M. Hester, *New York University: The Urban University Coming of Age* (New York: Newcomen Society, 1971), 21–23.

50. J. Martin Klotsche, *The Urban University and the Future of Our Cities* (New York: Harper & Row, 1966), 21.

51. Clarence Hilberry, "The Extension of the S.P.E. to Urban Universities," December 20, 1965, Ford Foundation Records, Education and Public Policy Record Group, series XV: James Armsey Subject Files, box 28, folder: Urban Universities.

52. John A. Dillon, "The Evolution of the American Urban University," *Urban Education* 15, no. 1 (1980): 40.

53. James Karabel, *The Politics of Structural Change in American Higher Education: The Case of Open Admissions at City University of New York* (Cambridge, MA: Huron Institute, 1981), 13.

54. Nathan Glazer, "City College," in *Academic Transformations: Seventeen Institutions Under Pressure*, ed. David Riesman and Varne A. Stedman for the Carnegie Commission on Higher Education (New York: McGraw-Hill, 1973), 90–98; Sheila C. Gordon, "The Transformation of the City University of New York, 1945–1970" (PhD diss., Columbia University, 1975), chap. 4.

55. James Traub, *City on a Hill: Testing the American Dream at City College* (Reading, MA: Addison-Wesley, 1994), 69–70; Robert E. Marshak, "Open Access, Open Admission, Open Warfare," *Change*, January/February 1982, 31.

56. Lewis S. Feuer, "The Stages in the Social History of Jewish Professors in American Colleges and Universities," *American Jewish History* 71, no. 4 (June 1982): 432–65.

57. Jerome Karabel, "Perspectives on Open Admission," *Educational Record* 53 (Winter 1972): 31.

58. Edward Quinn, "The Case for Open Admissions: 'We're Holding Our Own,'" *Change* 5, no. 6 (1974): 30–34.

59. Leonard Kriegel, *Working Through: A Teacher's Journey in the Urban University* (New York: Saturday Review Press, 1972), 209.

60. Quoted in Max Cohen, "Affirmative Action and Quotas," *Jewish Currents*, February 1974, 35.

61. Henry Wasser, "An American University and Universal Higher Education: The 'Open Admissions' System at C.U.N.Y.," *Higher Education* 2, no. 2 (May 1973): 154.

62. Martin Mayer, "Higher Education for All? The Case of Open Admissions," *Commentary*, February 1973, 45–47.

63. Nathan Glazer, "Are Academic Standards Obsolete?," *Change*, November/December 1970, 40.

64. Theodore I. Gross, "How to Kill a College: The Private Papers of a Campus Dean," *Saturday Review* 5, no. 9 (February 4, 1978): 14–15.

65. Mortimer Smith, "Varieties of Open Admissions," in *Open Admissions: The Pros and Cons*, ed. Jacques Barzun (Washington, DC: Council for Basic Education, 1972), 1–10; "Rutgers to Admit All Who Graduate in 3 N.J. Cities," *Chronicle of Higher Education*, March 21, 1969.

66. Regents of the University of the State of New York, *Minority Access to and Participation in Post-Secondary Education: A Statement of Policy and Proposed Action* (Albany: State of NY Education Department, May 1972), 11.

67. "Urban Planning for Public Officials," Ford Foundation Records, Projects (FA733), D-968: University of Chicago Program for Mayors and Councilmen, 1963.

68. *Annual Report of the Urban Internship Program-Urban Extension Service Conducted by Florida State University's Urban Research Center During the 1966–67 Fiscal Year* (Tallahassee: FSU Institute for Social Research, 1968), iii.

69. Letter from Gaylord Harnwell and Joesph Clark to Mitchell Svirdoff, September 10, 1969, Ford Foundation Records, National Affairs Division, Vice President, Office Files of Mitchell Sviridoff (FA577), series I: administrative subject files, P: University of Pennsylvania Center for Urban Research and Experiment, box 23, folder 2.

70. George Nash and Patricia Nash, *Survey of Activities in Urban and Minority Problems at the University of Pennsylvania* (New York: Columbia University Planning Committee, 1967), 46–49; "Improving the Information System for Cincinnati's Council," Charles F. Kettering Foundation Records, box 133, folder: University of Cincinnati, 1976–67, Hoover Institution Archives; "Workshops in Public Sector Labor Management Relations," Kettering Foundation Records, box 133, folder: University of Dayton, 1976–77.

71. Otto Feinstein and Jean Dietrick, "The City/University Consortium Experience in Detroit," *OECD Urban Management Studies* 5 [International Symposium, May 12–17, 1980] (1980): 113–19.

72. *Governing Urban Society: New Scientific Approaches* (Philadelphia: Philadelphia Academy of Political and Social Science, May 1967), vii, 60; *Long-Range Planning for Urban Research and Development: Technological Considerations* (Washington, DC: National Academy of Sciences, 1969); Anthony Walters, "A Way of Linking Technology with Urban Management" (1974), ACE Archives, box 705, folder 5.

73. George Spear, "The University and Adult Education," in *Universities in the Urban Crisis*, ed. Thomas P. Murphy (New York: Dunellen Publishing, 1975), 191.

74. Steven J. Diner, "The Land-Grant Analogy and the American Urban University: An Historical Analysis," *Journal of Metropolitan Universities* 23, no. 3 (March 2013): 61–76.

75. Glen C. Pulver, "Milwaukee," in *The Agony of the Inner City: What Can Continuing Education Do?*, ed. Stanley J. Drazek (College Park: University of Maryland, December 1967), 12–13; Glen C. Pulver, Daniel Schler and Lee J. Cary, *The Role of the University in Community Development* (Columbia: University of Missouri, 1969), 6–8.

76. Arthur J. Holland, "Newark," in Stanley J. Drazek, ed., *The Agony of the Inner City: What Can Continuing Education Do?* (College Park: University of Maryland, 1967), 17; *Boston University in the Community: A Report on the Metrocenter Survey of Community Involvement* (Boston, May 1967), 74; Kathleen Kilgore, *Transformations: A History of Boston University* (Boston: Boston University, 1991).

77. Otto Feinstein, *To Educate the People: An Experimental Model for Urban Higher Education for the Working Adult* (Detroit: Center for Urban Studies, Wayne State University, 1977), 9–12, 23.

78. Harry L. Miller, *New York University's Harlem Seminars* (New York: ERIC, 1967).

79. George E. Spear, "The University Public Service Mission," in Murphy, *Universities in the Urban Crisis*, 98.

80. James P. Pitts, "The Community Service Voucher Program: An Experiment in Community Access to University Resources," *Urban Affairs Quarterly* 13, no. 2 (December 1977): 181–206.

81. Nash and Nash, *Survey of Activities*, 42.

82. Andrew Schwebel et al., "University Extension in Urban Neighborhoods: A New Approach," *Journal of Higher Education* 47, no. 2 (March/April 1976): 206.

83. Robert C. Mason and Paul Roloff, "Preparing Professionals: Graduate Education for Lifelong Learning Roles in the City," in *The University and the Inner City: A Redefinition of Relationships*, ed. Franklin Spikes (Lexington, MA: Heath, 1980), 83.

84. James W. Wilson, "Cooperative Education: A Model of Mixing Work and Study," in *Student Personnel Work in Urban Colleges*, ed. Thomas F. Harrington (New York: Intext Educational Publishers, 1974), 223.

85. Gilbert A. Lowe Jr., "Howard University Students and the Community Service Project," *Journal of Negro Education* 36, no. 4 (Fall 1967): 368–76.

86. Preston L. Dent, Joint Educational Project: The University of Southern California's Partnership with the Community," in Spikes, *University and the Inner City*, 145–53.

87. Calvin B. T. Lee, "The Columbia College Citizenship Program: A Student Laboratory in Civic Affairs," *Journal of Higher Education* 36, 4 (April 1965): 186-94; Nash and Nash, *Survey of Activities*, 35.

88. Karen Duncan, *Community Action Curriculum Compendium* (Washington, DC: US National Student Association, November 15, 1968).

89. Martin Tarcher, "Higher Education: A Capital Gain," in *Vitality of the City*, 21.

90. "Racial Pressures on Urban Institutions," in Nichols and Mills, *Campus and the Racial Crisis*, 66.

91. Elden E. Jacobson, "Urban Curricula and the Liberal Arts College," *Liberal Education* 58, no. 2 (1972): 294.

92. *Directory of University Urban Research Centers* (Washington, DC: Urban Institute, 1969), 5.

93. Biles, *Fate of Cities*, 150–51.

94. James Banovetz, "College-Community Participation in Solving Urban Problems," in Roger W. Axford, ed., *College Community Consolidation*. Northern Illinois University, 1967, 1–3.

95. Stephen K. Bailey, "Urban Decision Making: The University's Role," in Cummings, *Political Backgrounds of Adult Education*, 11.

96. *Preliminary Report of the Committee on the University and the City* (Cambridge, MA: Harvard University, December 1968), 5.

97. "Gorham Criticizes Urban Institutes," *AUU Newsletter* 21, no. 1 (Winter 1969).

98. *Improving the Management of Urban Research: City/University Cooperation* (Paris: Organisation for Economic Co-operation and Development, 1980), 30–31.

99. W. G. Bennis, "The Role of the University in Restoring the Urban Habitat," *Educational Record* 55, no. 4 (Fall 1974): 223.

100. Dongbin Kim and John Rury, "The Rise of the Commuter Student: Changing Patterns of College Attendance for Students Living at Home in the United States, 1960–1980," *Teachers College Record* 113, no. 5 (2011): 1031–33.

101. Klotsche, *Urban University*, 104.

102. Richard F. Ward and Theodore E. Kurz, *The Commuting Student: A Study of Facilities at Wayne State University* (Detroit: Wayne State University, 1970), 10.

103. Reynold Feldman and Barbara A. Hursh, "Establishing an Urban Commuter University: The Need for Community," in Spikes, *University and the Inner City*, 1.

104. David Riesman, "The Urban University," *Massachusetts Review* 8 (1967): 484

105. Joseph Gusfield, Sidney Kronus, and Harold Mark, "The Urban Context and Higher Education: A Delineation of issues," *Journal of Higher Education* 41, no. 1 (January 1970): 39.

106. Herman P. Schuchman, "The Double Life of the Commuter College Student," *Mental Hygiene* 50, no. 1 (1966): 105, 110.

107. George D. Demos, "Problems of Integrating the Commuter College Student to the College Campus," *Journal of the American College Health Association* 15 (April 1967): 291–92.

108. Harrington, *Student Personnel Work*, 10.

109. J. E. Kysar, "Mental Health in an Urban Commuter University," *Archives of General Psychiatry* 2 (1964): 472–83.

110. Matthew Stark, "Commuter and Residence Hall Students Compared," *Personnel and Guidance Journal* 44, no. 3 (November 1965), 277–81.

111. Howard W. Graff and Gary R. Cooley, "Adjustment of Commuter and Resident Students," *Journal of College Student Personnel* 11, no. 1 (January 1970): 54–57.

112. Rickey I. George, "Resident or Commuter: A Study of Personality Differences," *Journal of College Student Personnel* 12, no. 3 (May 1971): 216–19.

113. See, for example, Martin Trow, "The Democratization of Higher Education in America," *European Journal of Sociology* 3, no. 2 (1962): 231–62; Earl McGrath, ed., *Universal Higher Education* (New York: McGraw-Hill, 1966); and W. Todd Furniss, ed., *Higher Education for Everybody? Issues and Implications* (Washington, DC: American Council on Education), 1971.

114. Klotsche, *Urban University*, 104.

115. McGrath, *Universal Higher Education*, xiii.

116. Robert E. Marshak, *Problems and Prospects of an Urban Public University* (New York: City College of New York, 1973), 192, 201.

117. Gordon D. Morgan, *The Ghetto College Student: A Descriptive Essay on College Youth from the Inner City* (Iowa City: American College Testing Service, 1970), 1, 5, 18.

118. Carl D. Peterson, "The Development and Achievement of Equal Opportunity Program Students," *Journal of College Student Personnel* 14, no. 1 (January 1973): 36–37.

CHAPTER FIVE: Government, Universities, and the Urban Crisis, 1964–1980

1. John F. Bauman, Roger Biles, and Kristin M. Szylvian, *The Ever-Changing American City, 1945–Present* (Lanham, MD: Rowman & Littlefield, 2012), chap. 3.

2. Peter Muirhead, "The 'Education Congress' and the Urban University," *AUU Proceedings* (1965): 15–23.

3. George E. Arnstein, "Model Cities: Colleges Can Reach Out to Troubled Cities with Action, Assistance, Analysis," *College and University Business*, September 1969, 51–63.

4. Roger Biles, *Fate of Cities: Urban America and the Federal Government, 1946–2000* (Lawrence: University Press of Kansas, 2011), chap. 5; Bauman, Biles, and Szylvian, *Ever-Changing City*, 123–24.

5. Thomas P. Murphy, ed., *Universities in the Urban Crisis* (New York: Dunellen Publishing, 1975), 60–61.

6. "Basic Information on HUD's University without Walls: National Urban Study Program," American Council on Education Archives, box 573, folder 11, Hoover Institution Archives, Stanford, CA.

7. Organization for Social and Technical Innovation, *Urban Universities: Rhetoric, Reality, and Conflict* (Washington, DC: US Department of Health, Education, and Welfare, Office of Education, 1970).

8. Murphy, *Universities in the Urban Crisis*, 62–70; Bernard Ross, *City-University Relations: From Coexistence to Cooperation* (Washington, DC: American Association for Higher Education, 1973), 16–17.

9. *A Strategic Approach to Urban Research and Development: Social and Behavioral Science Considerations* (Washington, DC: National Academy of Sciences, 1969), 1–6.

10. Robert C. Wood, "The Contributions of Political Science to Urban Form," in *Urban Life and Form*, ed. Werner Z. Hirsch (New York: Rinehart & Winston, 1963), 99–127.

11. Henry W. Maier, "An Overview of Urban Observatories," in *Governing Urban Society* (Philadelphia: American Academy of Political and Social Science, 1967), 216–19; Lawrence A. Williams, "The Urban Observatory Approach: A Decade of Conceptualization and Experimentation," *Urban Affairs Quarterly* 8 (September 1972): 6–7.

12. Thomas P. Murphy, "Public Administration Forum: The Urban Observatory Program," *Midwest Review of Public Administration* 1 (August 1971): 111–12; James A. Bayton, *Evaluation of the Urban Observatory Program* (Washington, DC: National Academy of Public Administration, 1971), 11.

13. William R. Barnes, "The Uses of Urban Research: A Perspective on the Urban Observatory Experience," *American Real Estate and Urban Economics Association* 2, no. 2 (1974): 47–58.

14. Clark Kerr, "The Urban-Grant University: A Model for the Future" (Phi Beta Kappa-Gamma Chapter Centennial Lecture) *City College Papers* 8 (1968): 5–6.

15. Ibid.; Clark Kerr, *Higher Education in the Troubled City* (Washington, DC: US Department of Health, Education and Welfare, 1968).

16. Organization for Social and Technical Innovation, *Urban Universities: Rhetoric, Reality and Conflict* (Washington, DC: US Office of Education, 1970), iii.

17. Donald Gerth et al., *The Urban Grant College: A College without Walls* (Los Angeles: Ombundsman Foundation, 1970), 3–4.

18. Carnegie Commission on Higher Education, *The Campus and the City: Maximizing Assets and Reducing Liabilities* (New York: McGraw-Hill, 1972), 4, 8, 118.

19. James C. Olson, "Proposed for Urban Universities: A Federal Urban Grant Program," *Phi Delta Kappan* 59, no. 1 (September 1977): 21–22.

20. Ibid.; Maurice Berube, *The Urban University in America* (Westport, Conn.: Greenwood, 1978), 176.

21. *Urban Grant University Act: Hearings before the Subcommittee on Postsecondary Education of the Committee on Education and Labor, House of Representatives, 95th Congress on HR7328* (Washington, DC: Government Printing Office, 1979), 549–50.

22. Ibid.

23. Lewis B. Mayhew, "The Town Gown Campus," in *The Vitality of a City: Challenge to Higher Education* (San Francisco: University of California San Francisco Medical Center, 1967), 12–13.

24. Ralph D. Gray, *IUPUI—The Making of an Urban University* (Bloomington: Indiana University Press, 2003), chap. 8.

25. Richard M. Freeland, *Academia's Golden Age: The Universities in Massachusetts, 1945–1970* (Oxford: Oxford University Press, 1992), 6.

26. J. Martin Klotsche, *The University of Wisconsin–Milwaukee: An Urban University* (Milwaukee: University of Wisconsin–Milwaukee, 1972), 78–81; Harrington address, *AUU Proceedings* 54 (1966): 23–27.

27. Kenneth H. Ashworth, "Urban Renewal and the University: A Tool for Campus Expansion," *Journal of Higher Education* 35, no. 9 (December 1964): 493–96.

28. Albert Solnit, "Town and Gown: One Community," *Teachers College Record*, January 1967, 289–94.

29. "Colleges Learn Their Urban ABCs," *Business Week*, June 1, 1968, 94–97.

30. Fred M. Hechinger, "The Urban University," *New York Times*, May 3, 1968.

31. "Confrontation: The Campus and the City," *Change*, January/February 1969, 7–18.

32. Joseph Gusfield, Sidney Kronus, and Harold Mark, "The Urban Context and Higher Education: A Delineation of Issues," *Journal of Higher Education* 41, no. 1 (January 1970): 29–43.

33. Kermit C. Parsons and Georgia K. Davis, "The Urban University and Its Urban Environment," *Minerva* 9 (July 1971): 361–85.

34. Quoted in Joanne Grant, *Confrontation on Campus: The Columbia Pattern for the New Protest* (New York: Signet, 1969), 29.

35. Ibid., 28–29; Jerry Avorn, *Up against the Ivy Wall: A History of the Columbia Crisis* (New York: Atheneum, 1969), 12–15.

36. George and Patricia Nash, *Survey of Activities in Urban and Minority Problems at the University of Pennsylvania* (New York: Columbia University Planning Committee, 1967), 73–76.

37. "Report to the President of the University of Pennsylvania Regarding Future Policies and Actions on Dormitory Operations and Dining Services," Academy for Educational Development Records, box 53, Hoover Institution Archives.

38. Robert L. Carroll, Hayden B. May, and Samuel V. Noe, *University-Community Tension and Urban Community Form* (Cincinnati, OH: University of Cincinnati, 1972), 1:44–49.

39. Robert A. McCaughey, *Stand Columbia: A History of Columbia University in the City of New York, 1974–2004* (New York: Columbia University Press, 2003), 545–48.

40. Themis Chronopoulos, "Urban Decline and the Withdrawal of New York University from University Heights, the Bronx," *Bronx County Historical Society Journal* 46, no. 1–2 (2009): 5–24.

41. Raymond Schroth, *Fordham: A History and Memoir* (New York: Fordham University Press, 2008), 323.

42. Ibid., 323–29; Debra Caruso Marrone, *Fordham University and the United States: A History* (New York: E-Lit Books, 2013), 194–95.

43. Paul C. Reinert, "Saint Louis University's Role as Midwife to Urban Rebirth," *AGB Reports* 24, no. 5 (September/October 1982): 24–28.

44. Charles K. Hyde, "Brief History of Wayne State University," in *History of Wayne State University in Photographs*, ed. Evelyn Aschenbrenner (Detroit: Wayne State University Press, 2009), 10–12.

45. Nicholas Varga, *Baltimore's Loyola, Loyola's Baltimore, 1851–1986* (Baltimore: Maryland Historical Society, 1990), 430–37, 497–98, 527–29.

46. Bill Carey, *Chancellors, Commodores, and Coeds: A History of Vanderbilt University* (Nashville, TN: Clearbrook Press, 2003), 315.

47. Ibid., 315–20.

48. "Resolution Relative to City of Milwaukee Opposition to Further Expansion of the University of Wisconsin–Milwaukee," June 2, 1969, UW–Milwaukee Office of the Chancellor Records, series 1: Klotsche Administration Records, box 14, folder 3, University of Wisconsin–Milwaukee Archives.

49. Robert Curvin, *Inside Newark: Decline, Rebellion, and the Search for Transformation* (New Brunswick, NJ: Rutgers University Press, 2014), 118–27.

50. See Christopher Klemek, *The Transatlantic Collapse of Urban Renewal: Postwar Urbanism from New York to Berlin* (Chicago: University of Chicago Press, 2011); Biles, *Fate of Cities*; and Jon Teaford, *The Rough Road to Renaissance: Urban Revitalization in America, 1940–1985* (Baltimore: Johns Hopkins University Press, 1990).

CHAPTER SIX: The Legacy of the Urban Crisis and the Ever-Changing City, 1981–2016

1. Howard P. Chudacoff, Judith E. Smith, and Peter C. Baldwin, *The Evolution of American Urban Society*, 8th ed. (Boston: Pearson, 2015), 221.

2. University of Virginia Demographics Research Group, "The Changing Shape of America's Metro Areas," http://statchatva.org/changing-shape-of-american-cities/.

3. Anne Habiby and Allen Amirkhanian, "Urban Universities and Inner City Revitalization—An Action Agenda for Leaders and Practitioners," *Metropolitan Universities* 14, no. 4 (December 2003): 31–33.

4. *Leveraging Colleges and Universities for Urban Economic Revitalization: An Action Agenda* (Boston: Initiative for a Competitive Inner City; CEOs for Cities, 2001), 2.

5. Richard Florida, *The Rise of the Creative Class, Revisited* (New York: Basic Books, 2012), viii, 309–12.

6. Paul C. Brophy and Rachel D. Godsil, *Retooling HUD for a Catalytic Federal Government: A Report to Secretary Shaun Donovan* (Penn Institute for Urban Research, February 2009), 141.

7. Amanda Wittman and Terah Crews, *Engaged Learning Economies: Aligning Civic Engagement and Economic Development in Community-Campus Partnerships* (Boston: Campus Compact, 2012), 6.

8. Ernest Spaights, "Toward a Definition of an Urban University," *Urban Review* 15, no. 3 (October 1980): 372. See also Ernest Spaights, Harold Dixon, and Susanne Nickolai, "Issues and Problems of the Urban University," *Urban Review* 17, no. 1 (1985): 25–32.

9. S. Richardson Hill Jr., "Urban Universities: Twentieth-Century Phenomena," *Phi Beta Kappa Journal National Forum* 61, no. 3 (1981): 38–39.

10. Thomas N. Bonner, "The 'Distinctly' Urban University: A Bad Idea?," *Chronicle of Higher Education*, September 23, 1981.

11. Address by Ronald Williams in *The Urban University: Present and Future*, University of Arkansas at Little Rock Monograph Series (Little Rock: University of Arkansas, 1981), 9, 12.

12. Arnold Grobman, *Urban State Universities: An Unfinished National Agenda* (New York: Praeger, 1988), 9.

13. Sheldon Hackney, "Reinventing the American University: Toward a University System for the Twenty-First Century," *Teachers College Record* 95, no. 3 (Spring 1994): 311–16.

14. Mary H. Mundt, "The Urban University: An Opportunity for Renewal in Higher Education," *Innovative Higher Education* 22, no. 3 (Spring 1998): 252.

15. Erin McNamara Horvat and Kathleen M. Shaw, "Redefining Campus: Urban Universities and the Idea of Place," *New Directions in Higher Education* 105 (Spring 1999): 101–7.

16. Davis L. Stocum, "Urban Universities: A Model for the 21st Century," *Vital Speeches of the Day* 66, no. 23 (September 15, 2000): 715–18.

17. Harold Enarson, "The 'Distinctly Urban' University: A Bad Idea?," *Chronicle of Higher Education*, September 23, 1981.

18. David Adamany, "The University as Urban Citizen," *Educational Record* 73, no. 2 (Spring 1992): 6–9, and "Sustaining University Values While Reinventing University Commitments to Our Cities," *Teachers College Record* 95, no. 3 (Spring 1994): 324–31.

19. Nevin Brown, *Urban Universities and National Urban Policy: Report on a Meeting of Urban University Presidents and Chancellors* (Washington, DC: NASULGC, July 1982), 1.

20. Andrew Rudnick, *The American University in the Urban Context: Status Report and Call for Leadership* (Washington, DC: NASULGC, 1983), 27–29.

21. Charles E. Hathaway, Paige E. Mulhollan, and Karen A. White, "Metropolitan Universities: Models for the Twentieth-First Century," *Metropolitan Universities* 1, no. 1 (Spring 1990): 9–20.

22. Hathaway, Mulhollan, and White, "Metropolitan Universities," 13.

23. Ibid., 12–13.

24. *Returning to Our Roots: Executive Summaries of the Reports of the Kellogg Commission on the Future of State and Land-Grant Universities* (Washington, DC: NASULGC, January 2001), 13–14.

25. Jeffrey Cantor, *Experiential Learning in Higher Education: Linking Classroom and Community*, AAHE-ERIC Higher Education Reports, 1995 no. 7 (Washington, DC: Graduate School of Education and Human Development, George Washington University, 1995).

26. Robert G. Bringle and Julie A. Hatcher, "Implementing Service Learning in Higher Education," *Journal of Higher Education* 67, no. 2 (March/April 1996): 221.

27. From http://compact.org/who-we-are.

28. George Kuh et al., *Student Learning outside the Classroom: Transcending Artificial Boundaries*, ASHE-ERIC Higher Education Reports, 1994 no. 8 (Washington, DC: US Department of Education, Office of Educational Research and Improvement, Educational Resources Information Center, 1994); Cantor, *Experiential Learning in Higher Education*; John Saltmarsh and Edward Zlotkowski, eds., *Higher Education and Democracy: Essays on Service Learning and Community Engagement* (Philadelphia: Temple University Press, 2011); Barbara Jacoby, *Service-Learning in Higher Education: Concepts and Practices* (San Francisco: Jossey-Bass, 1996).

29. Anne Colby and Thomas Ehrlich, "Introduction: Higher Education and the Development of Civic Responsibility," in *Civic Responsibility and Higher Education*, ed. Thomas Ehrlich (Washington, DC: American Council on Education, 2000), vii.

30. Barbara Jacoby and Associates, eds., *Civic Engagement in Higher Education: Concepts and Practices* (San Francisco: Jossey-Bass, 2009), 10–23.

31. Lorilee R. Sandmann, Courtney H. Thornton, and Audrey J. Jaeger, eds., *Institutionalizing Community Engagement in Higher Education: The First Wave of Carnegie Classified Institutions*, New Directions for Higher Education, no. 147 (San Francisco: Jossey-Bass, 2009), 1–3; Carnegie Community Engagement Website, New England Resource Center for Higher Education, www.nerche.org.

32. Jacoby, *Civic Engagement*, 12.

33. Jake New, "Colleges Placing Increasing Importance on Programs Promoting Civic Engagement," *Inside Higher Education*, May 10, 2016.

34. "Setting Municipal Priorities," Rockefeller Brothers Fund Archives (FA005), RG 3.1 (Projects [Grants]), box 239, folder 1519, Rockefeller Archive Center, Sleepy Hollow, NY; Clyde Haberman, "Koch to Boycott Meeting on City to Avoid Critics," *New York Times*, November 18, 1981.

35. "The Urban Research Center of New York University," Foundation Center of New York records (FA023), Charles H. Revson Foundation, box 1376, Rockefeller Archive Center.

36. "Detailed Progress Report: The Urban Family Life Project," June 29, 1988, Carnegie Corporation of New York Archives, Carnegie Corporation Archives, series III.A (Grants), box 1117, Columbia University Rare Book and Manuscript Library, New York; William Julius Wilson, *The Truly Disadvantaged: The Inner City, the Underclass, and Public Policy* (Chicago: University of Chicago Press, 1987).

37. Foundation for Child Development Records (FA421), series 1 (Grants), box 7, Rockefeller Archive Center.

38. Nathan Glazer, "Facing Three Ways: City and University in New York Since World War II," in *The University and the City: From Medieval Origins to the Present*, ed. Thomas Bender (New York: Oxford University Press, 1988), 267–89.

39. Ira Harkavy, "The University and the Social Sciences in the Social Order: An Historical Overview and 'Where Do We Go From Here?,'" *Virginia Social Science Journal* 27 (1992): 2.

40. Adamany, "Sustaining University Values," 326.

41. Thomas Bender, "Scholarship, Local Life, and the Necessity of Worldliness," in *The Urban University and Its Identity*, ed. Herman Van Der Wusten (Dordrecht: Kluwer Academic, 1998), 21.

42. Engagement Scholarship Consortium, https://engagementscholarship.org.

43. "History of the Lynton Award," New England Resource Center for Higher Education, http://www.nerche.org/index.php?option=com_content&view=article&id=26&Itemid=100.

44. "Community-Engagement Scholarship Awards," APLU, http://www.aplu.org/projects-and-initiatives/economic-development-and-community-engagement/community-university-engagement-awards/.

45. Ryan Stellabotte, "Lending Hope: The University Neighborhood Housing Program," *Fordham Magazine* 35, no. 1 (Fall 2001): 1–21; Deborah Caruso Marrone, *Fordham University and the United States: A History* (New York: E-Lit Books, 2013), 203.

46. Katherine S. Morgan, "A Campus Battles to Rid Its Neighborhood of Crime," *Chronicle of Higher Education*, November 13, 1991; Martin Van Der Werf, "Urban Universities Try New Ways to Reach Out to Their Communities," *Chronicle of Higher Education*, April 30, 1999.

47. John L. Puckett and Mark Frazier Lloyd, *Becoming Penn: The Pragmatic American University, 1950–2000* (Philadelphia: University of Pennsylvania Press, 2015), chap. 9–10; Ira Harkavy and John L. Puckett, "The Role of Mediating Structures in University and

Community Revitalization: The University of Pennsylvania and West Philadelphia as a Case Study," *Journal of Research and Development in Education* 25, no. 1 (Fall 1991): 16–19; Sheldon Hackney, "The University and Its Community: Past and Present," *Annals of the American Academy of Political and Social Science* 488 (November 1986): 141–43; Judith Rodin, *The University and Urban Revival: Out of the Ivory Tower and into the Streets* (Philadelphia: University of Pennsylvania Press, 2007).

48. Stephen A. Sterrett, "Planning and Partnerships for the Renewal of Urban Neighborhoods," *Journal of Higher Education Outreach and Engagement* 13, no. 3 (2009): 113; Sayoni Bose, "Universities and the Redevelopment Politics of the Neoliberal City," *Urban Studies* 52, no. 14 (2015): 2616–32.

49. Angela Fowler-Young, "The Process of Developing a University Neighborhood in a Downtown Urban Environment: Baltimore's University Center" (presented at Society for College and University Planning conference, July 26, 1994).

50. Richard M. Freeland, "Universities and Cities Need to Rethink Their Relationships," *Chronicle of Higher Education*, May 13, 2005.

51. Beadle Moore, introduction to *Urban University: Present and Future*, 1–3.

52. Andrew Young, "Public Expectations of Higher Education beyond 1984," *AASCU Studies* 2 (1985): 8.

53. Ezra Bowen, David Jackson, and Michael Riley, "Those Hot Colleges on the Climb," *Time Magazine*, April 28, 1986.

54. Wim Wievel and David Broski, "The Great Cities Institute: Dilemmas of Implementing the Urban Land Grant Mission," *Metropolitan Universities* 10, no. 1 (Summer 1999): 29–38.

55. Peggy Gordon Elliott, *The Urban Campus: Educating the New Majority for the New Century* (Phoenix, AZ: Oryx, 1994), 146.

56. *Colleges and Communities: Gateway to the American Dream* (Washington, DC: HUD Office of Policy Development and Research, Summer 2000), i.

57. Henry G. Cisneros, *The University and the Urban Challenge* (Washington, DC: HUD, February 1995), 14–16.

58. Ibid., 2.

59. Avis Vidal, *Lessons from the Community Outreach Partnership Center Program: Final Report* (Washington, DC: Urban Institute), i–viii.

60. Cisneros, *University and the Urban Challenge*, 14–15; Lauri Alpern and Joni Lee, "Building an Engaged Institution: The HUD Community Outreach Partnership Program," *Metropolitan Universities* 10, no. 4 (Spring 2000): 33–42.

61. *Urban Universities: Anchors Generating Prosperity for America's Cities* (Washington, DC: Coalition of Urban Serving Universities, 2010), 21–23; "USU Releases Report on Impact Urban Universities Have on Local Communities," *A Public Voice: APLU's Online Newsletter*, September 7, 2010.

62. Caitlin Moran, "At Temple University, the City Is the Classroom," *Chronicle of Higher Education*, November 28, 2008.

63. Seth Zweifler and Jonah Newman, "Elite Institutions: Far More Diverse than They Were 20 Years Ago," *Chronicle of Higher Education*, November 1, 2013.

64. Jeffrey Selingo, "Location, Location, Location: Urban Hot Spots Are the Place to Be," *Chronicle of Higher Education*, August 1, 2014.

65. Claire Zillman, "These Are the Best Cities for College Students," *Fortune.com*, November 23, 2015.

66. Address by Ronald Williams in *Urban University: Present and Future*, 10–11.

67. Pastora San Juan Cafferty and Gail Spangenberg, *Backs against the Wall: Urban-Oriented Colleges and Universities and the Urban Poor and Disadvantaged*, Series on Higher Education in the Cities (New York: Ford Foundation, 1983), 5–11.

68. Evelyn M. Davila, *Today's Urban University Students*, part 1, *Profile of a New Generation* (New York: College Entrance Examination Board, 1985), 1, and part 2, *A Case Study of Hunter College* (New York: College Entrance Examination Board, 1985), 4–5.

69. Elliott, *Urban Campus*, xii.

70. Larry H. Dietz and Vicky L. Triponey, eds., *Serving Students at Metropolitan Universities: The Unique Opportunities and Challenges* (San Francisco: Jossey-Bass, 1997).

71. Barbara Jacoby, "Engaging First-Year Commuter Students in Learning," *Metropolitan Universities* 15, no. 2 (June 2004): 12–30.

72. Mary Jean Thomas remarks, in *Urban University: Present and Future*, 25.

73. Spaights, Dixon, and Nickolai, "Issues and Problems of Urban University," 28.

74. James Traub, *City on a Hill: Testing the American Dream at City College* (Boston: Addison-Wesley, 1994), vii.

75. Patrick Healy, "Can City College Restore Its Luster by Ending Open Admission?," *Chronicle of Higher Education*, July 7, 2000.

76. John L. Pulley, "Brick by Brick, an Urban University Rebuilds Its Campus and Alumni Ties," *Chronicle of Higher Education*, July 20, 2001.

Bibliographic Essay

Historians of American higher education have written relatively little about the development of urban colleges and universities' relationship to cities until quite recently. There are, however, two histories of municipal universities. In 1932, the US Office of Education published *The History of the Municipal University in the United States* by R. H. Eckelberry from Ohio State University, and in 1962 the Center for Applied Research in Education published *The Municipal University* by William S. Carlson, president of the University of Toledo. An early edited collection devoted to urban universities is Peter Sammartino and Willis Rudy, *The Private Urban University: A Colloquium* (Fairleigh Dickinson University Press, 1966). Thomas Kaluzynski's "An Historical View of the Concept of the Urban University" (PhD diss., University of Illinois, 1975) explored the evolving definition of the urban university. Richard Angelo examined the urban students' perspective in "The Students at the University of Pennsylvania and the Temple College of Philadelphia, 1873–1906," *History of Education Quarterly* 19, no. 2 (1979). Gene D. Lewis and Zane L. Miller also looked at the issue of definition in "Charles W. Dabney and the Urban University: An Institution in Search of a Mission, 1904–1914," *Cincinnati Historical Society Bulletin* 38, no. 3 (Fall 1980). George Rosen published a valuable specialized study of the politics behind the creation of the University of Illinois at Chicago in *Decision Making Chicago Style: The Genesis of a University of Illinois Campus* (University of Illinois Press, 1980). The earliest scholarly publication about the Association of Urban Universities appeared in James Crooks, "The AUU and the Mission of the Urban University," *Urbanism Past and Present* 7, no. 4 (Summer/Fall 1982).

Since 2000, several scholars have examined aspects of urban university history. Margaret Pugh O'Mara, *Cities of Knowledge: Cold War Science and the Search for the Next Silicon Valley* (Princeton University Press, 2005), assessed the impact of post-1945 scientific and military research at universities on the economies of the San Francisco peninsula, Philadelphia, and Atlanta. John Louis Recchuiti looked at the role of social scientists in Progressive Era reform in *Civic Engagement: Social Science and Progressive Era Reform in New York City* (University of Pennsylvania Press, 2007), addressing issues similar to those I studied in *A City and Its Universities: Public Policy in Chicago, 1892–1919* (University of North Carolina Press, 1980). And Sharon Harr, *The City as Campus: Urbanism and Higher Education in Chicago* (University of Minnesota Press, 2011), offered a broad history of higher education's use of the city for teaching, in particular how Chicago's universities interfaced with urban renewal and the city's physical development.

Numerous leaders in higher education have written books about the importance of urban universities. In 1928, Parke Rexford Kolbe, president of the Polytechnic Institute of Brooklyn, authored *Urban Influences on Higher Education in England and the United States* (Macmillan), a study done in conjunction with the American Association for Adult Education and with support from the Carnegie Foundation. But most of this writing came in the mid-1960s and thereafter, addressing the "urban crisis." University of Wisconsin–Milwaukee chancellor J. Martin Klotsche, who vigorously advocated the need for universities in cities, spelled out his argument *in The Urban University: And the Future of Our Cities* (Harper & Row, 1966). The 1970s saw publication of two similarly titled edited collections, University of Pennsylvania psychology professor Howard E. Mitchell's *The University and the Urban Crisis* (Behavioral Publications) and University of Maryland political scientist Thomas Murphy's *Universities in the Urban Crisis* (Dunellen Publishing, 1975), as well as *The Urban University in America* (Greenwood Press, 1978), written by Maurice Berube, a scholar of educational leadership at Old Dominion University. Other volumes by university presidents or chancellors included Ronald Williams, "Northeastern Illinois University," in *The Urban University: Present and Future* (University of Arkansas at Little Rock, 1981); Arnold Grobman (University of Missouri–St. Louis), *Urban State Universities: An Unfinished National Agenda* (Praeger, 1988); and Peggy Gordon Elliott, *The Urban Campus: Educating the New Majority for the New Century* (Oryx Press, 1994). Elliott was an AASCU senior fellow when she wrote her book; a few years later she became president of South Dakota State University. An invaluable primary source on the history of universities and cities is the *Proceedings of the Annual Meeting of the Association of Urban Universities*, published most years between 1914 and 1977.

There is a rich scholarly literature on the history of American higher education. Although not specifically focused on institutions' relationship with cities, it provides a crucial context for scholars interested in urban colleges and universities. Historical surveys, many now viewed as classics, include Frederick Rudolph, *The American College and University: A History* (Vintage, 1962); Allen Nevins, *The State Universities and Democracy* (University of Illinois Press, 1962); Laurence R. Veysey, *The Emergence of the American University* (University of Chicago Press, 1965); Christopher Lucas, *American Higher Education: A History* (St. Martin's Press, 1994; 2nd ed., 2006); John Thelin, *A History of American Higher Education* (Johns Hopkins University Press, 2004; 2nd ed., 2011); and Roger Geiger, *The History of American Higher Education: Learning and Culture from the Founding to World War II* (Princeton University Press, 2015).

Helen Lefkowitz Horowitz, *Alma Mater: Design and Experience in the Women's Colleges from the Nineteenth-Century Beginnings to the 1930s* (Knopf, 1984); explores the history of women's colleges. The role of philanthropy in the development of American higher education is reviewed in Merle Curti and Roderick Nash, *Philanthropy in the Shaping of American Higher Education* (Rutgers Press, 1965), and in John R. Thelin and Richard W. Trollinger, *Philanthropy and American Higher Education* (Palgrave Macmillan, 2014). Hugh Hawkins surveys the development and influence of higher education organizations in *Banding Together: The Rise of National Associations in American Higher Education, 1887–1950* (Johns Hopkins University Press, 1992). Harold S. Wechsler, *The Qualified Student: A History of Selective College Admissions in America* (John Wiley, 1977; expanded ed., Transaction, 2014), traces the complex process by which colleges determined whom they should teach and how it changed over time.

The history of teacher education is examined by Christine Ogren, *The American Normal School: "An Instrument of Great Good"* (Palgrave Macmillan, 2005), and James Fraser, *Preparing America's Teachers: A History* (Teachers College Press, 2007). Christopher P. Loss, *Between Citizens and the State: The Politics of American Higher Education in the 20th Century* (Princeton University Press, 2012), focuses on the growing involvement of the federal government in higher education and the conservative opposition to it since World War I. On the history of campus design, see Paul Venable Turner, *Campus: An*

American Planning Tradition (MIT Press, 1984), and Blake Gumprecht, *The American College Town* (University of Massachusetts Press, 2008).

Several historical studies focus on specific time periods. Among these are Earl Dudley Ross, *Democracy's College: The Land-Grant Movement in the Formative Stage* (Iowa State College Press, 1942); Roger Geiger, ed., *The American College in the Nineteenth Century* (Vanderbilt University Press, 2000); Charles M. Vest, *The American Research University: From World War II to the World Wide Web* (University of California Press, 2007); and David O. Levine, *The American College and the Culture of Aspiration, 1915–1940* (Cornell University Press, 1986). Roger Geiger also has published two books on the development of the research university, *To Advance Knowledge: The Growth of American Research Universities, 1900–1940* (Oxford University Press, 1986; repr., Transaction Publishers, 2004) and *Research and Relevant Knowledge: American Research Universities since World War II* (Oxford University Press, 1993).

Some scholars have written about the history of religious groups in American higher education, particularly in cities. Studies of Catholics universities, which were mostly located in cities, include Paul Reinert, *The Urban Catholic University* (Sheed & Ward, 1970); Edward J. Powers, *Catholic Higher Education in America: A History* (Appleton-Century-Crofts, 1972); and William P. Leahy, *Adapting to America: Catholics, Jesuits, and Higher Education in the Twentieth Century* (Georgetown University Press, 1991). Sherry Gorelick has examined Jewish college students in *City College and the Jewish Poor: Education in New York, 1880–1924* (Rutgers University Press, 1981). The experience of African American students in the mid-1960s and early 1970s is explored by Ibram H. Rogers, *The Black Campus Movement: Black Students and the Racial Reconstitution of Higher Education, 1965–1972* (Palgrave Macmillan, 2012).

Several volumes by social scientists written during the "urban crisis" era provide useful perspectives on universities and cities in that period, as well as on higher educational institutions across the nation. Among these are Christopher Jencks and David Riesman, *The Academic Revolution* (Doubleday, 1968; 2nd ed., Transaction, 2002); George Nash, ed., *The University and the City: Eight Cases of Involvement* (McGraw-Hill, 1973); and David Riesman and Verne Stadtman, eds., *Academic Transformation: Seventeen Institutions under Pressure* (McGraw-Hill, 1973).

There are, of course, innumerable histories of individual universities, usually published by universities themselves, and often quite celebratory. The ones I found most useful in writing this book, listed chronologically by publication date, are Rudy S. Willis, *The College of the City of New York: A History, 1847–1947* (City College Press, 1949); Samuel White Patterson, *Hunter College: Eighty-Five Years of Service* (Lantern Press, 1955); Edward Potts Cheyney, *History of the University of Pennsylvania, 1740–1940* (University of Pennsylvania Press, 1940); Thomas Evans Coulton, *A City College in Action: Struggle and Achievement at Brooklyn College, 1930–1955* (Harper Brothers, 1955); Hugh Hawkins, *Pioneer: A History of Johns Hopkins University, 1874–1899* (Cornell University Press, 1960); Rayford W. Logan, *Howard University: The First Hundred Years, 1867–1967* (NYU Press, 1969); J. Martin Klotsche, *The University of Wisconsin–Milwaukee: An Urban University* (University of Wisconsin–Milwaukee, 1972); C. H. Cramer, *Case Western Reserve: A History of the University, 1826–1976* (Little, Brown, 1976); Murray M. Horowitz, *Brooklyn College: The First Half-Century* (Brooklyn College Press, 1981); Charles F. Donovan, David Dunigen, and Paul A. Fitzgerald, *History of Boston College: From the Beginning to 1990* (University Press of Boston College, 1990); Nicholas Varga, *Baltimore's Loyola, Loyola's Baltimore, 1851–1986* (Maryland State Historical Society, 1990); Ralph Gray, *IUPUI—The Making of an*

Urban University (Indiana University Press, 2003); Robert A. McCaughey, *Stand Columbia: A History of Columbia University in the City of New York, 1754–2004* (Columbia University Press, 2003); Thomas Jablonsky, *Milwaukee's Jesuit University: Marquette, 1881–1981* (Marquette University Press, 2007); Raymond A. Schroth, *Fordham: A History and Memoir* (Fordham University Press, 2008); Harold S. Wechsler, "Brewing Bachelors: The History of the University of Newark," *Paedagogica Historica* 46, no. 1–2 (2010); John L. Puckett and Mark Frazier Lloyd, *Becoming Penn: The Pragmatic American University, 1950–2000* (University of Pennsylvania Press, 2015); and John W. Boyer, *The University of Chicago: A History* (University of Chicago Press, 2015).

A large number of works, mostly written in the decade following the start of open admissions in the early 1970s, address open admission at the City University of New York. These include Sheila Gordon, "The Transformation of the City University of New York: 1945–1970" (PhD diss., Teachers College, Columbia University, 1975); David A. Trivett, *Open Admissions and the CUNY Experience* (ERIC, 1976); and Ben R. Williams, *Open Admissions at the City University of New York 1970: Its Implications for Higher Education* (ERIC, 1977). The National Institute of Education's Project on Politics and Inequality in American Higher Education supported Jerome Karabel's work, *The Politics of Structural Change in American Higher Education: The Case of Open Admissions at the City University of New York* (Huron Institute, 1981). Several CUNY faculty wrote about their experiences, often very critically: Leonard Kriegel, *Working Through: A Teacher's Journey in the Urban University* (Saturday Review Press, 1972); L. G. Heller, *The Death of the American University: With Special Reference to the Collapse of City College of New York* (A. S. Barnes, 1976); Geoffrey Wagner, *The End of Education* (A. S. Barnes, 1976); Theodore L. Gross, *Academic Turmoil: The Reality and Promise of Open Education* (Doubleday, 1980); and David E. Lavin et al., *Right versus Privilege: The Open Admissions Experiment at the City University of New York* (Free Press, 1981). Journalist James Traub provides a detailed account of open admission at City College in *City on a Hill: Testing the American Dream at City College* (Addison-Wesley, 1994), which he wrote after spending eighteen months on the campus. Harold S. Wechsler, *The Qualified Student* (see above) also offers a detailed history of access issues at CUNY.

Sociologist Martin A. Trow wrote extensively over many years about democratization and open access to higher education in the United States and abroad. His publications on this subject written before the launch of CUNY open admissions include "The Democratization of Higher Education in America," *European Journal of Sociology* 3, no. 2 (1962), and *The Democratization of Higher Education in America* (Bobbs-Merrill, 1967). He subsequently published *The Expansion and Transformation of Higher Education* (General Learning Press, 1972); *Problems in the Transition from Elite to Mass Higher Education* (McGraw-Hill, 1973); "'Elite Higher Education': An Endangered Species?," *Minerva* 14, no. 3 (Autumn 1976); "Academic Standards and Mass Higher Education," *Higher Education Quarterly* 41, no. 3 (1987); "Class, Race, and Higher Education in America," *American Behavioral Scientist* 35, no. 4–5 (March–June 1992); "From Mass Higher Education to Universal Access: The American Advantage," *Minerva* 37 (Spring 2000); and many other articles and books. Many of his writings on this subject are republished, each with a commentary by a different scholar, in *Martin Trow: Twentieth-Century Higher Education: Elite to Mass to Universal*, ed. Michael Burrage (Johns Hopkins University Press, 2010).

David Lavin, the CUNY faculty member who wrote *Rights versus Privilege* (see above), co-authored two other books on open admission and access: with David Hyllegard, *Changing the Odds: Open Admissions and Life Chances of the Disadvantaged* (Yale University Press, 1996), and, with Paul Atwell, *Passing the Torch: Does Higher Education for the Disadvantaged*

Pay Off across the Generations? (Russell Sage Foundation, 2007). Other works on college access nationally include Philip R. Rever, *Open Admissions and Equal Access* (American College Testing Program, 1971); Kim Dongbin and John L. Rury, "The Changing Profile of College Access: The Truman Commission and Enrollment Patterns in the Postwar Era," *History of Education Quarterly* 47, no. 3 (August 2007); and Scott M. Gelber, *Courtrooms and Classrooms: A Legal History of College Access, 1860–1960* (Johns Hopkins University Press, 2016).

To place the history of urban higher education in the context of American urbanization, I have drawn heavily on the extensive US urban history literature. The history of American cities is extremely complex, so no survey can discuss everything. Some surveys of American urban history do not consider any aspect of the role of universities in the development of American cities; others devote some attention to the rise of urban research or the role of particular universities in neighborhood economic development and revitalization. Among these surveys are Charles N. Glaab and A. Theodore Brown, *A History of Urban America* (3rd ed., Macmillan, 1983); Zane L. Miller and Patricia M. Melvin, *The Urbanization of Modern America: A Brief History* (2nd ed., Harcourt Brace Jovanovich, 1987); Raymond A. Mohl, *The Making of Urban America* (SR Books, 1997); David R. Goldfield and Blaine A. Brownell, *Urban America: A History* (2nd ed., Houghton Mifflin, 1990); Howard P. Chudacoff, Judith E. Smith, and Peter C. Baldwin, *The Evolution of American Urban Society* (8th ed., Pearson, 2015); Lisa Kristoff Boehm and Steven M. Corey, *America's Urban History* (Routledge, 2015); and Jon C. Teaford, *The Twentieth-Century American City: Problems, Promise, and Reality* (3rd ed., Johns Hopkins University Press, 2016). John Bauman, Roger Biles, and Kristin Szylvian, in *The Ever-Changing American City: 1945–Present* (Rowman & Littlefield, 2012), discuss the role of universities in the development of urban research and in the economic growth of some cities. Given the long-standing practice of building enclosed urban campuses with trees and park-like qualities, I found the history of urban parks helpful, particularly the classic work by Roy Rosenzweig and Elizabeth Blackmar, *The Park and the People: A History of Central Park* (Cornell University Press, 1992).

Two books on the history of federal policy toward cities were very useful: Mark Gelfand, *A Nation of Cities: The Federal Government and Urban America, 1933–1965* (Oxford University Press, 1975), and Roger Biles, *The Fate of Cities: Urban America and the Federal Government* (University Press of Kansas, 2011). Given higher education's history of anti-urbanism, Steven Conn, *Americans against the City: Anti-Urbanism in the Twentieth Century* (Oxford University Press, 2014), proved extremely helpful, as did its predecessor, Morton White and Lucia White's intellectual history of anti-urbanism, *The Intellectual Versus the City: From Thomas Jefferson to Frank Lloyd Wright* (Harvard University Press, 1962).

Writings about the condition of American cities since the 1980s address substantially the role of universities, their students, and their faculties in facilitating the urban revitalization in the new information- and technology-driven economy. Richard Florida, *The Rise of the Creative Class* (Basic Books, 2002; rev. ed., 2011), argues that economic development now requires highly educated and creative people who increasingly cluster in cities, giving universities in urban areas the opportunity to play a key role in economic development. Alexander von Hoffman, *House by House, Block by Block: The Rebirth of America's Neighborhoods* (Oxford University Press, 2003), discusses at length the role of the Illinois Institute of Technology in reshaping the Bronzeville section of south Chicago and also shows the role of the knowledge economy in neighborhood revitalization in the Bronx, Boston, Atlanta, and Los Angeles. Arnold Hirsch, *Making the Second Ghetto: Race and Housing in Chicago, 1940–1960* (Cambridge University Press,1985), also examines the role of universities, along with many other forces, in creating highly segregated black neighborhoods in Chicago.

Studies of gentrification in American cities, a process often connected with higher education institutions, include John Palen and Bruce London, *Gentrification, Displacement, and Neighborhood Revitalization* (SUNY Press, 1984); Neil Smith, *The New Urban Frontier: Gentrification and the Revanchist City* (Routledge, 1996); Lance Freeman, *There Goes the 'Hood: Views of Gentrification from the Ground Up* (Temple University Press, 2006); Japonica Brown-Saracino, *A Neighborhood Never Changes: Gentrification, Social Preservation, and the Search for Authenticity* (University of Chicago Press, 2009); and Suleiman Osman, *The Invention of Brownstone Brooklyn: Gentrification and the Search for Authenticity in Postwar New York* (Oxford University Press, 2012).

The historical literature on urban renewal is important in understanding neighborhood development activities of many universities. Books on this subject include E. Michael Jones, *The Slaughter of Cities: Urban Renewal as Ethnic Cleansing* (St. Augustine's Press, 2004); Christopher Klemek, *The Transatlantic Collapse of Urban Renewal: Postwar Urbanism from New York to Berlin* (University of Chicago Press, 2011); and Derek S. Hyra, *The New Urban Renewal: The Economic Transformation of Harlem and Bronzeville* (University of Chicago Press, 2008).

A good deal of recent scholarship examines the role of universities in urban renewal. See John Ingram Gilderbloom, *Promise and Betrayal: Universities and the Battle for Sustainable Urban Neighborhoods* (SUNY Press, 2005); Harley F. Etienne, *Pushing Back the Gates: Neighborhood Perspectives on University-Driven Revitalization in West Philadelphia* (Temple University Press, 2012); Michael Carriere, "Chicago, the South Side Planning Board, and the Search for (Further) Order: Toward an Intellectual Lineage of Urban Renewal in Postwar America," *Journal of Urban History* 39, no. 3 (May 2013); LaDale Winling, "Students and the Second Ghetto: Federal Legislation, Urban Politics, and Campus Planning at the University of Chicago," *Journal of Planning History* 10, no. 1 (2011); and Davarian L. Baldwin, "The '800-Pound Gargoyle': The Long History of Higher Education and Urban Development on Chicago's South Side," *American Quarterly* 67, no. 1 (March 2015).

In short, until quite recently historians of American higher education have devoted relatively little attention to universities' relationship to their home cities. However, the extensive historical writing on the history of American higher education and on US urban history illuminate the broad context in which urban higher education has evolved.

Index

Page numbers in *italics* refer to photos.